This book is due for return on or before the last date shown below.

C 5 MAY 2011

05 MAY 2011

2 0 FEB 2012

2 8 FEB 2013

11 JUN 2014   1 0 JUN 2015

2 6 MAY 2016

1 1 NOV 2016

WITHDRAWN

&

E

n

fe

Don Gresswell Ltd., London, N21   Cat. No. 1207

...IA AND POPULAR
CULTURE by BURTON,
GRAEME

Hodder & Stoughton

A MEMBER OF THE HODDER HEADLINE GROUP

ACKNOWLEDGEMENTS

The writing of books rests in a cradle of support from colleagues, editors and family. I am grateful to colleagues at the University of the West of England for their indirect support through conversation – my learning environment. I want to thank my editors, especially Paul Selfe and Llinos Edwards, for their help and suggestions in the distillation of a large subject area. They have always been positive and patient. And closest to home I want to thank Judy for discussion, and for listening when she might have preferred to have been doing something else.

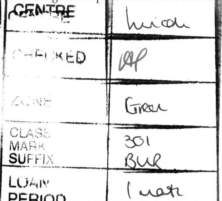

Orders: please contact Bookpoint Ltd, 39 Milton Park, Abingdon, Oxon OX14 4TD. Telephone: (44) 01235 400414, Fax: (44) 01235 400454. Lines are open from 9.00–6.00, Monday to Saturday, with a 24 hour message answering service. Email address: orders@bookpoint.co.uk

A catalogue record for this title is available from The British Library

ISBN 0 340 747064

First published 1999
Impression number 10 9 8 7 6 5 4 3 2
Year   2005 2004 2003 2002 2001 2000

Cover image: *Audience*, Diana Ong. Superstock.

ry, England.
& Stoughton Educational, a division of
ad, London NW1 3BH by Redwood Books,

CONTENTS

1

INTRODUCTION

HOW TO USE THE BOOK

EACH CHAPTER IN this book examines one or more of the central debates relating to the sociology of media. The text is devised for readers with little or no background knowledge in the subject, and there are Study Points and Activities throughout to encourage a consideration of the issues raised. Student readers are advised to make use of these and answer them either on paper or in group discussion, a particularly fruitful way of learning; they will assist them to develop the skills of interpretation, analysis and evaluation. There are many ways of preparing for an exam, but a thorough understanding of the material is obviously crucial.

Each chapter is structured to give a clear understanding of the authors, concepts and issues that you need to know about. To assist understanding and facilitate later revision, it is often helpful to make concise notes.

MAKING NOTES FROM THE BOOK

Linear notes
- Bold headings establish key points: names, theories and concepts.
- Subheadings indicate details of relevant issues.
- A few numbered points list related arguments.

Diagram or pattern notes
- Use a large blank sheet of paper and write a key idea in the centre.
- Make links between this and related issues.
- Show also the connections between sub issues which share features in common.

Both systems have their advantages and disadvantages, and may take some time to perfect. Linear notes can be little more than a copy of what is already in the book and patterned notes can be confusing. But if you practise the skill, they can reduce material efficiently and concisely becoming invaluable for revision. Diagrammatic notes may be very useful for those with a strong visual memory and provide a clear overview of a whole issue, showing patterns of interconnection. The introduction of helpful drawings or a touch of humour into the format is often a good way to facilitate the recall of names, research studies and complex concepts.

Activity

- Make a diagram to show the two ways of making notes with their possible advantages and disadvantages

SKILLS ADVICE

Students must develop and display certain skills for their examination and recognise which ones are being tested in a question. The clues are frequently in key words in the opening part. The skill domains are:

1 **Knowledge and understanding:** the ability to discuss the views of the main theorists; their similarities and differences; the strengths and weaknesses of evidence. To gain marks students must display this when asked to *explain, examine, suggest a method, outline reasons.*
2 **Interpretation, application and analysis:** the use of evidence in a logical, relevant way, either to show how it supports arguments or refutes them. Students must show this ability when asked *identify, use items A/B/C, draw conclusions from a table.*
3 **Evaluation:** the skill of assessing evidence in a balanced way so that logical conclusions follow. Students can recognise this skill when asked to *assess, critically examine, comment on levels of reliability, compare and contrast,* or if asked *to what extent.*

Activity

Draw an evaluation table, as below, using the whole of an A4 page. Examine studies as you proceed in your work and fill in the relevant details. Keep it for revision purposes.

Sociologist			
Title of the study		Strengths	Weaknesses
Verdict			
Judgement/justification			

REVISION ADVICE

- Keep clear notes at all times in a file or on disk (with back up copy).
- Be familiar with exam papers and their demands.
- Become familiar with key authors, their theories, their research and sociological concepts.

Activity

Make and keep **Key Concept Cards**, as shown below.

COLLECTIVE CONSCIENCE

Key idea

A term used by **Durkheim** meaning:

- The existence of a social and moral order exterior to individuals and acting upon them as an independent force.
- The shared sentiments, beliefs and values of individuals which make up the **collective conscience.**
- In **traditional societies** it forms the basis of social order.
- As societies modernise the collective conscience weakens: **mechanical solidarity** is replaced by **organic solidarity**.

Key theorist: Emile Durkheim

Syllabus area: Functionalism

EXAMINATION ADVICE

To develop an effective method of writing, answers should be:

- **Sociological:** use the language and research findings of sociologists; do not use anecdotal opinion gathered from people not involved in sociology to support arguments.

- **Adequate in length:** enough is written to obtain the marks available.
- **Interconnected** with other parts of the syllabus (such as stratification, gender, ethnicity).
- **Logical:** the answer follows from the relevant evidence.
- **Balanced:** arguments and counter arguments are weighed; references are suitable.
- **Accurate:** reliable data is obtained from many sources.

The three skill areas on p 2 should be demonstrated, so that the question is answered effectively.

In displaying knowledge, the student is not necessarily also demonstrating interpretation.

- This must be specified with phrases like 'Therefore, this study leads to the view that…'
- Sections of answers should hang together, one leading to the next. This shows how the question is being answered by a process of analysis based on the evidence.
- Reach a conclusion based on the evidence used and the interpretations made.

The skill of evaluation is often regarded (not necessarily accurately) as the most problematic. Evaluation means being judge and jury; the strengths and weaknesses of evidence is assessed and an overall judgement about its value is made. To evaluate an argument or theory, consider whether it usefully opens up debate; explains the events studied; does it have major weaknesses?

Activity
Look through some past examination papers and pick out the evaluation questions. Underline the evaluation words and work out which skills are required.

COURSEWORK ADVICE

Coursework provides an opportunity to carry out a study using primary and/or secondary data to investigate an issue of sociological interest, and must address theoretical issues. The suggestions included at the end of each chapter may be adapted or used to generate further ideas. Final decision must be agreed with a teacher or tutor.

MAKING A PLAN

Before starting a piece of coursework, you should make a plan:

1 Read and make notes from articles describing research projects in journals.
2 Have a clear aim in mind; choose an issue that interests you and is within your ability.
3 Decide more precisely what you want to know; establish a simple hypothesis to test.
4 Select a range of possible methods; consider both quantitative and qualitative.
5 Decide on a range of possible sources of information.
6 List the people to whom you can seek help, perhaps including a statistician.

WRITING THE PROJECT

1 Seek frequent advice from a teacher or tutor.
2 Check the weighting for different objectives in the marking scheme.
3 Keep clear notes throughout, including new ideas and any problems that arise.
4 Limit its length (maximum 5,000 words).
5 Label and index the study in the following way:
   a **Rationale:** a reason for choosing the subject; preliminary observations on the chosen area
   b **Context:** an outline of the theoretical and empirical context of the study
   c **Methodology:** a statement of the methodology used and reasons for selecting it
   d **Content:** presentation of the evidence and/or argument including results
   e **Evaluation:** the outcomes are weighed and strengths and weaknesses noted.
   f **Sources:** all the sources of information are listed.
OR
   a **Title**
   b **Contents**
   c **Abstract:** a brief summary of the aims, methods, findings and evaluation.
   d **Rationale**
   e **The Study**
   f **Research Diary**
   g **Bibliography**
   h **Appendix:** to include proposal for the study, single examples of a questionnaire or other data-gathering instrument and transcripts of interviews.
   i **Annex:** to include raw data gathered.

Paul Selfe
Series editor

2

WHAT IS MEANT BY THE MASS MEDIA?

Introduction

THIS CHAPTER LOOKS at:

- how we may define the media and their history
- concepts about the media
- different critical approaches to making sense of the ways in which the media have developed.

WHAT DO WE MEAN BY 'MEDIA'?

It is generally understood that the term 'media' covers means of communication such as the press, broadcasting and cinema. This book leads on these examples. However, there is a wide range of other media that bring various kinds of entertainment and information to large audiences – magazines or the music industry.

There are also industries which support the activities of the media, even if they don't communicate directly with the public: the Press Association supplies news, Screen Services makes trailers for films, Gallup provides market research. Then there are the telecommunication industries which 'carry' material for the media – cable or satellite. For our purposes, it will be assumed that 'media' refers to institutions or businesses which communicate to audiences, mainly in the provision of leisure/entertainment.

It should be remembered that the media do *mediate* – ie they reconstruct source material in various ways, for various reasons, mainly to make it attractive to the audience.

Table 1: *Theorists, concepts, key phrases and propositions in this chapter*		
THEORISTS	CONCEPTS KEY PHRASES	PROPOSITIONS
Brian Winston	Media history as about technology	● The interaction between societal change and technological change
James Curran and Jean Seaton	Media history as about institution and change	● Issues of power and the interaction between media institutions and government
Dennis McQuail	Media theories	● A description of general elements of media theory, eg institution, audience, effect
Jean Seaton	Institutions, power and responsibility	● The media as an agency of social control
James O'Halloran et al.	Social context	● How events are reported and predicted within a social framework
David Barrat	Audience, content, form, context	● The development of media analysis from institution to form to audience
Raymond Williams	Economic determinants	● Factors affecting media output
David Morley	Audience, class, reading texts	● How different audiences respond to different material
Philip Schlesinger	Professionalism (news)	● The values of news gatherers and editors: the institutional context
Greg Philo et al.	Text, analysis (news)	● The value of content analysis: the measurement of bias
D Strinati and S Wagg	Popular culture	● The relationship between cultural politics and party politics
David Morley, Pierre Bourdieu	Postmodernism	● The rejection of certainties about media influence and notions of reality

All this raises general key questions:

● Who controls the media, and with what effect?

- How and why do they construct their products?
- Who are the audiences?
- What effects do these products have on the audiences?
- In whose interests do the media operate?

WHAT IS MEDIA HISTORY?

Ideas about what 'history' is will vary according to the critical perspective of the historian. It can be 'read', for example, as being about the exercise of political power, or about processes of social change, or in terms of the situation of specific social groups such as women or ethnic minorities.

In effect, history is about information and interpretation.

- *Information* is about evidence from primary and secondary sources. Primary sources might be an interview with a film producer, or a copy of the 1991 Broadcasting Act. This is first-hand information. Secondary sources might be any example of media material – a magazine or a TV programme. This is second hand because it comes from the producers, the institution. We may deduce things from reading a newspaper article, but this is not the same as talking to the reporter and editor who originally produced it.
- *Interpretation* is about the sense one makes of that evidence, the theories that are constructed about the significance of the information.

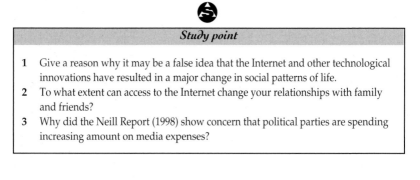

Study point

1   Give a reason why it may be a false idea that the Internet and other technological innovations have resulted in a major change in social patterns of life.
2   To what extent can access to the Internet change your relationships with family and friends?
3   Why did the Neill Report (1998) show concern that political parties are spending increasing amount on media expenses?

Dominant approaches to media history which also relate to dominant theories about the media summarised elsewhere in this chapter, have focused on the following points:

- the nature and growth of media power (in media institutions), including management and control of the media;
- the changing relationship of media institutions with government;
- the nature of technological developments in the media as they affect other items in this list, including media products;

Table 2: The development of the press and broadcasting: selected key aspects

	1950s	1960s	1970s	1980s	1990s
The press	• Decline in circulation – impact of radio and then television • Pre-war patterns of 'family' ownership	• Arrival of Murdoch – *The Sun* – and sensational tabloid format. He also buys *The Times* and *News of the World*	• Takeovers – new corporate ownership, eg Black – *The Telegraph* • Circulation stabilises • Influence of press on political process and electioneering • Polarisation of quality and tabloid markets • Increasing power of new proprietors, eg Murdoch and Maxwell	• Tabloid circulation wars • *Independent* started 1986 • Issues surrounding Falklands coverage 1982	• Debates over intrusive reporting (eg Princess Diana) • Gulf War coverage
Broadcasting	• Commercial TV brings competition to BBC plus American imports • ITA and successors are set up to control commercialism • ITV genre programming hits BBC • Start of pop music shows • Debates about ITV – commercial values • Suez Crisis – news challenges government • Radio in a rut with old-fashioned entertainment – Light programmes	• Expansion of TV channels and genres including news • Rise of TV drama and drama documentary – realism, eg *Z Cars* • Impact of TV on presentation of sport • Video recording brings repeats • Advertising income exceeds that of the press • Greater use of films to fill expanding air time • Revamp of old-fashioned radio channels in face of declining audience • TV satire with political edge – TV looking at its own culture	• Commercial local radio arrives – expansion of local and regional services • TV consolidates practices • Competitive programming • Increasing dominance of films, soaps and game shows • Debates about TV as a duopoly • News images of industrial action undermine Labour government	• Thatcher gets tough with BBC – reorganises on a more commercial basis • Competition from new cable/satellite channels • C4 started – debates about nature of PSB • Decline of TV play and rise of costume drama and mini series • Impact of documentary images leads to Live Aid • Impact of VCRs on viewing habits • Rise of independent production houses • Average weekly viewing hours now = 26	• Broadcasting Act benefits independent production and revamps regulation of channels • Loosening of takeover rules brings concentration of power – eg Carlton • Rise of TV documentary forms engaging real lives and events – *Police 5* • Radio dominated by talk and music formats – 'serious' audience declines • National commercial radio starts

Patterns of change:
- **Institutions:** concentration of ownership; globalisation of operations; accumulation of power
- **Technology:** partial displacement of one medium by another; collaboration between one medium and another
- **Product:** the diversification and reworking of generic forms
- **Audience:** increasing fragmentation; targeting by paper or channel
- **Political:** social perceptions of politics framed by media and personalised; mutual exploitation by politicians and media

Table 3: Media history – institutions, products, distribution: the 1950s onwards

	TELEVISION	RADIO	MUSIC/AUDIO	PRESS/PRINT	CINEMA
1950s	• Coronation (1953) establishes TV as popular medium • Commercial TV arrives (1954) • First election coverage (1959) • Belson Report (1959): first criticism of effects of TV on family life	• Radio as background medium • Light and serious channels, but waning force in news and light entertainment – falling audiences • Radio Luxembourg attracts the youth audience	• Rock and roll • First TV music shows • Domestic record players • Traditional jazz fad	• Stagnation – many dailies losing money	• The decline of Hollywood studios • Experiments with screen formats
1960s	• Pilkington Report (1961): expansion of educational TV, and controls over commercial TV • BBC2 (1964) – minority programming • *News at 10* (1967) – innovations • Pictures from the Moon (1969)	• Pirate radio, Caroline (1964) • BBC radio revamped – 1, 2, 3, and 4 and local (1967) • Rise of music formats and young audience	• Rise of English bands – Beatles and Stones. R & B influence • Young audience for new radio channels	• Loss of leftwing press, eg *Herald* • Rise of new girls' magazines (eg *Jackie*) • Arrival of Murdoch – new tabloid journalism, *The Sun* (1964) • New music papers • First Sunday mags	• Majors bought by corporations • Star power as star system ends
1970s	• Open University BBC2 (1971) • Restrictions on broadcasting hours lifted 1972 • Annan Report (1976) preserves PSB ideal • Complaints about violence on TV (cop series) bring in guidelines • Rise of global co-productions	• Commercial local radio – ILR (1972) • General expansion of local radio • Car radios become common	• Motown, Glam Rock • Music movies (eg *Grease*) • Dominance of corporations (Polygram) • Rise of Indies – eg Island – and Reggae • New folk music • Rise of stadium and festival performance	• *TV Times* and *Radio Times* biggest-selling magazines • Dominance of tabloids • Takeovers concentrate power	• Rise of the blockbuster • Low point in audience attendance • Majors dominate British distribution and exhibition • Rise of power of marketing
1980s	• Falklands War (1982) – furore over reporting and government control • Channel 4/S4C (1982) • Breakfast TV (1983) • Sky satellite TV (1984) • Peacock Report (1986) criticises BBC but preserves licence fee	• New wave of pirate radio, including in ethnic communities • Growth of hospital and community radio	• Great variety of music genres and media/events dedicated to these • Techno and dance music • Rise of new club scene	• Rise of powerful proprietors and editors, eg Maxwell and Mirror Group • First paper (*Today*) produced by electronic compositing (1985) • Move out of Fleet Street (1986) – union power broken, new technology established	• Impact of video market • Development of multiplexes • Rise of youth films and that market
1990s	• Broadcasting Act (1991) requires 25% independent production • Takeovers concentrate power in commercial sector • Channel 5 (1997)	• Radio 5 (1990) • Commercial national radio eg Classic FM (1992), Virgin (1993) • Talk Radio (1995) and rise of talk format	• Influence of black and Asian music – bangra/rap/jungle	• Tabloid sensationalism and attacks on leftwing councils	• Japanese buy Universal and Columbia

- changes in media products and forms, especially in relation to kinds of realism;
- changes in censorship of media, in relation to changing social attitudes and to ideas about media effects;
- changes in representations of social groups within media products;
- the relationship between social change and media products, including the rise of marketing and the creation of a youth audience;
- the growth of media operations, also in relation to media genres.

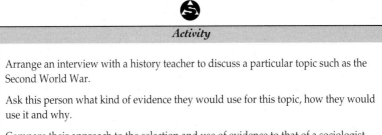

Activity

Arrange an interview with a history teacher to discuss a particular topic such as the Second World War.

Ask this person what kind of evidence they would use for this topic, how they would use it and why.

Compare their approach to the selection and use of evidence to that of a sociologist, especially with regard to media evidence such as film or audio recordings from that period. Draw up a list of similarities and differences in the two approaches.

KEY CONCEPTS IN MEDIA AND CULTURAL STUDIES

Study of the media is located within a range of disciplines – communication, gender, media, cultural studies, as well as sociology.

Sociology is particularly interested in:

- the nature of audiences (and subcultural groups)
- media effects
- representations
- theories of media in relation to society
- the power exerted by media institutions over society (and as a part of it)
- news and bias
- ideology, and ideas about how it may operate through the media.

More generally, there are a number of common key words in media study, which overlap with the previous list. These are sometimes known as *keys concepts in media*. It will be useful now to describe these so that you understand their significance when they come up later in this book.

IDEOLOGY

- This refers to dominant ideas about the nature and operation of power relationships in culture and society.
- It also refers to dominant beliefs and values which are taken for granted.

A key issue here is about ways in which various aspects of media contribute to the continuation of those beliefs and values without their being questioned. For example, much media material suggests the importance of romance, marriage and weddings: it implicitly approves of these three elements. The wedding of Prince Charles and Princess Diana in 1981 was a major cultural event commercially syndicated round the world. Also, ironically as it turns out, it was a powerful endorsement of the value of these three elements.

FORM

- This refers to the ways in which media products such as films or newspapers are put together.
- It also refers to the ways in which qualities such as realism are constructed.

A key issue here is the extent to which this construction shapes and distorts the social meanings generated by the product. For example, the introduction to many TV news programmes influences our perception of their truthfulness through the symbolism of logos and through the face-on shots and big desks of power.

NARRATIVE

- This refers to that aspect of form which has to do with the construction of story and drama.
- It can be argued that a news article tells a story as much as does a novel.

A key issue here is how narrative shapes meaning. For example, many narratives (whether of the news or of fiction) incorporate conflict between people, but often really between opposing ideas. The effect might be to define, say, social deprivation within a story in terms of conflict – perhaps in terms of those who resist their deprived situation as opposed to those who do not. This definition may be simplistic and may conceal the social practices which lead to the deprivation behind the story.

TEXT

- This refers to all media products as if they are 'books', drawing attention to the fact that they can all be 'read' for their meanings.

A key issue here is how texts may or may not be read differently by different audiences, and why. In cultural studies' terms, the wedding event (see 'ideology' above) would be as much a text for reading as could the magazine wedding photograph.

GENRE

- This refers to the fact that most media products fall into categories or types.

A key issue here is how these repetitive categories may also repeat social meanings and social practices. For example, much television crime drama repeats a view that criminal activity is exciting (if wrong) and that detection is dominated by the use of technology. Neither of these views is generally true in the everyday experience of police officers.

REPRESENTATION

- This refers to media presentations of social groups, categorised in many ways – by gender, ethnicity, age, class, among others.
- The concept covers not only specific types (old women) but also collective types (the elderly), and possibly institutions/conditions (old age, old people's homes).
- All these things can be represented, often repetitively, and may communicate dominant meanings (see 'ideology').

A key issue here is to what extent the representation is positive or negative. For example, a film such as *Born on the Fourth of July* makes an attempt to tackle issues around disablement in a fairly constructive way, whereas partially disabled villains in films such as *Judge Dredd* represent an unhappy association of ideas about being disabled.

AUDIENCE

- This refers to definable groups of people who consume media products.
- An audience may be defined in terms of social groupings – women for romantic fiction, or young males for computer games.

A key issue here would be how far the audience's own perception of its social group (and its other cultural experiences) affects its preferences for and readings of the very material which is targeted at it. For example, do young women see themselves as having a gender and generation position which makes it 'appropriate' for them to read magazines such as *More* or *Sugar*? Or do they construct their sense of social position through reading these magazines?

EFFECTS

- This refers to propositions about how and why media products affect audiences.

A key issue here is how far audiences are passive or active in terms of making sense of the media. For example, are film viewers to be seen as bags into which cultural meanings from a film are stuffed? Or are they to be seen as critical predators, plundering what amuses and interests them, and throwing the rest of the film-viewing experience away?

INSTITUTION

- This refers to the organisations which run and control the media.

This includes service institutions such as Reuters news agency which supplies material for world news services.

A key issue here is about the consequences of the way that these institutions operate along lines which maintain the interests of capital(ism) but ignore the interests of certain sections of the community (such as the unemployed). For example, many women's magazines operate in conjunction with fashion and cosmetics industries to represent a lifestyle based on consumption of goods which the unemployed cannot always afford.

Study point

1   Why do the producers of a TV programme such as *Top of the Pops* make and broadcast the programme?
2   Why do the viewers watch it?
3   What do you learn about the values and interests of institutions and audiences from the answers to these questions?

CRITICAL APPROACHES IN THE DEVELOPMENT OF MEDIA AND CULTURAL STUDIES

There are a number of ideas about media studies in relation to:

- how it has developed
- concepts in media and cultural studies
- the growth of the media themselves.

David Barrat (1986) acknowledges the work of **Dennis McQuail** and of Curran and Seaton in describing three stages in the development of media studies, all with some emphasis on the idea of effects:

1   *until 1940*: during which it was believed, largely on the basis of Marxist criticism developed by the Frankfurt School, that the media affect audiences as a mass; that they could produce conformist behaviour; and that they undermine culture (assumed to be the high cultural pursuits of the elite);
2   *from 1940 to 1965*: during which it came to be accepted that the media probably do not have short-term behavioural effects on the audience (although the

popular press still clings to this notion!). It was believed that effects were conditioned by social influences on the audience (see Chapter 7);

3 *from 1965 to 1985*: during which the emphasis shifted from effects and the social context of the audience to looking at the content and form of media products (representation, for example).

It may be added that since then there has developed a particular interest in audience reception and cultural context, with the growth of cultural studies.

Curran and Seaton (1997) start media critical history with a survey of the Frankfurt School and notions of the power of press and broadcasting. This chapter leads through areas of institution and audience to comment on the media as an agency of social control, referring to **Pierre Bourdieu**'s comments on the education system as fulfilling the same function.

They look at the media in terms of the idea of *process*. This means that they take an *interactionist* approach centering on the relationship between institution, products and audience. They are also interested in views of the connection between media functions, political events and social change.

Raymond Williams (1974) looks at the way in which television and its technology have become the dominant medium of popular culture. It relates the medium to the concepts of high culture and 'low' culture, and to debates in the 1950s and 1960s about what constitutes 'proper' culture. His views are driven by the notion of *economic determinants* shaping the way that institutions produce the popular culture of television, which itself becomes a *social institution*.

James O'Halloran et al. (1970) looks at the reporting of the demonstrations against the Vietnam War, which took place in Grosvenor Square, London in 1968. It examines not just the partiality of news coverage of the event, but also the notion of *social context*. The writers draw attention to the commitment of media resources to coverage – to a prediction that the demonstration *had to be* an event. They also examine the police as an institution, and argue that as a social grouping the police has evidently conservative views about social behaviour and social control. Such views would inevitably put the police at odds with the radical position of the demonstrators. This is also seen in the context of establishment support for the war.

McQuail (1983) argues that there are three basic elements to all media theory, not least if one wishes to examine the relationship between mass communication and social change over a period of time:

1 communication technology
2 the form and content of media material
3 social changes themselves – referring to social structures, the development of institutions and shifts in public beliefs and attitudes.

The relationship between media culture and society: four key terms

	MEDIA	Direction of effect	SOCIETY
TERMS			
Idealism	————————————————▶		
Materialism	◀————————————————		
Interdependence	◀———————————————▶		
Autonomy		none	

SOURCE: AFTER MCQUAIL (1983)

In particular, McQuail takes up the argument about whether media culture influences society (social structures) or vice versa.

He offers four key terms (see the diagram):

1 **interdependence**: this suggests a dynamic relationship between the two elements in which the one inevitably affects the other;
2 **idealism**: this refers to the conviction that media do affect society, not least through the effect of their technologies;
3 **materialism**: this argues that society is shaped by political and economic forces, and that media may have some part in this, but that media are more a reflection of change and shaping;
4 **autonomy**: this suggests that there is no necessary relationship between media and society.

One example of the 'idealistic belief' that the media do affect society is that of the pit bull terrier scare in 1993. Television and the press took up stories about children being mauled or even killed by these dogs. Demands for action followed, including from some MPs, and ill-conceived legislation was rushed through to have this breed killed or neutered.

Greg Philo (and the Glasgow Media Group (1976, and successive books analysing news coverage) looks at news as *text* for analysis, not least in terms of meanings and effects, of structural principles and semiotics. It also takes a *content analysis* approach, measuring proportions of content or kinds of treatment in order to weigh up their significance. The work of the Glasgow Media Group has continued for many years, and depends on the recording and evaluation of hours of broadcast news.

Dominic Strinati and **Stephen Wagg** (1992) represent another approach to media theory and history which is less concerned with macro models of the relationship between media and society than it is with popular culture, often with very specific examples of material. They describe three areas of interest for their book which are a fair picture for cultural studies as a whole:

1 the relationship between popular culture and social differences
2 texts and contents – the range of popular cultural forms
3 historical contexts for the growth of popular culture.

David Morley (1992) looks at the history of audience studies in one chapter and at debates about the nature of audience and effects generally. In particular, the history chapter discusses the notion that effects on audiences may be seen in terms of class: that the subculture of the audience and the codes of communication which it uses are crucial in defining how it decodes media material.

He also writes on postmodernism in a chapter in Morley et al. (ed.) 1996. It is the postmodernist's view that there can be no objective truth or reality about the way that people interpret the social world. There are only relative interpretations of reality, which are defined through advertising and other forms of popular culture. With the rapid expansion of media channels, the worlds that people inhabit are increasingly artificial. It is suggested that media and cultural studies should look at style (ie form) and at meanings drawn from style.

Morley argues that we have moved from a period of modernist theories about mass audiences to a situation where one needs to talk about *narrowcasting* and specific audiences. He talks about the effects of technology in enabling media to target these audiences. This is tied up with a kind of ironic and referential style (ie form). For example, a current advert for a chocolate product uses characters who were heroes of a 1950s Western series (the Lone Ranger and Tonto). It raises interesting questions about whom the advert is aimed at and how it will be understood. Morley also talks about the rejection of certainties in discussing the nature of media and their effects – the kinds of certainties about media effects on mass audiences and society which characterised writing from the 1930s to the 1950s.

Table 4: *Common propositions in media sociology with some reference to media/cultural studies*

- The media have created mass audiences, and have an effect on these audiences
- The media may be seen as an agency of social control
- Effects of the media on audiences depend on social conditions
- Media material contains representations which affect ideas about social groups
- There is a relationship between the mass media and social change
- The development of media technology relates to developments in society
- There is a relationship between media popular culture and social identities/social differences
- Popular media culture may be best understood in its social context
- The study of (media) culture is bound up with an understanding of dominant structures and dominant views within our society

In a small group, examine a copy of a magazine for young women, such as *More*.

1 Discuss what it says about the values and cultural interests of young women readers (this refers to the ideas of text and meaning).

2 Arrange interviews with women in their forties/fifties. Give them a chance to look at the copy of the magazine before you discuss it with them. Base your interview on points which have come out of your discussion. But in particular ask them to comment on how the magazine might have been received when they were your age (this refers to the idea of changing social context).

SUMMARY

The term 'media' applies to the entertainment and information products of the media industries, as well as to examples of telecommunications which help bring those products to us.

There are various ideas about what media history is and how to approach it. It may be summarised as being about key words such as institution, product and audience, as well as about the social changes which relate to these factors.

To understand the media (and their development), one needs to use these key words and to understand how they connect with issues about media construction and influence.

There have been various critical approaches to media study in the development of critiques of the media. These have variously put emphasis on understanding media producers and businesses, on media texts and their construction, and on media audiences and social context.

In the development of media study, criticism has moved from believing that the media do things to people, to looking at what people do with the media, and at the actual media material. An interest in effects of the media has been a constant factor as media study has progressed. This is important in sociological critiques of the media. However, those taking a cultural studies approach would argue that effects are largely unprovable, and that it is more useful to concentrate on text, social context and social groups.

STUDY GUIDES

Group work

1 One view of the development of the media is that it pivots on understanding cultural experiences.
   a Work in groups to compare your experiences of watching children's television.
   b Identify programmes watched by a number of your group. Write down reasons as to why those programmes were watched. Discuss what you now think those programmes implied about social behaviour, gender behaviour, social groups.
2 Divide yourselves into two subgroups and brainstorm reasons for and against the idea that there are or are not connections between media and particular social groups/social behaviours.

Compare your two lists of reasons and discuss their validity and whether or not you can reach any firm conclusions.

Practice questions

1 In what ways has the globalisation of media businesses and their activities brought more power to media institutions?
2 Curran and Seaton take an interactionist approach to the history of broadcasting and the press. What does this mean in terms of evaluating the relationship between media and society?
3 In what ways may a survey of TV programmes reveal 'social differences' or differences between social groups?

Coursework suggestions

1 Investigate different experiences of the media in different periods of time by, for example, researching the radio listening habits of your grandparents' generation when they were young, as compared with the experiences of young people today. Focus on the changing content and treatment (ie form) of the material, as well as on preferred programmes and reasons for listening.

Evaluate the implications of what you find out in terms of how media may or may not have changed and how they may affect audiences.

2 **Peter Golding** uses a supply–demand model to describe media development. Investigate new examples of media supplying a demand for leisure/entertainment on the part of the public, and those factors in society which have led to an increase in leisure activities generally. Do your investigations suggest that either the media or social pressures lead these developments?

3

WHAT IS MEANT BY POPULAR CULTURE?

Introduction

THIS CHAPTER IS about:

- what we understand by the term culture
- key concepts used to interpret the production, use and significance of popular culture
- debates or key questions raised about popular culture
- categories of theorising about popular culture, such as Marxism
- key commentators, within these categories, on popular culture.

NOTIONS OF CULTURE

It may be said that culture is about the distinctiveness of social groups which gives them an identity. The media are significant in representing that identity to others, as well as to the given cultural group. Sociologists are interested in the norms and values which inform the actions of a group, in the meanings which are attached to those actions, and in the products possessed by the group which also have meanings attached to them.

Critiques of culture also come out of the norms and values of those who construct that critique. This is much the same as arguing that it is difficult or next to impossible to comment on ideology except from other ideological positions.

Table 5: *Theorists, concepts, key phrases and propositions in this chapter*

THEORIST	CONCEPTS KEY PHRASES	PROPOSITIONS
Walter Benjamin	Cultural production	• Mass production and creation of mass communication to mass audience
Theodor Adorno	Commodities/fetishism	• Goods acquire a cultural value beyond their material price
Antoni Gramsci	Hegemony	• Exertion of power and control by one class over others
Raymond Williams	High culture/low culture Structures of feeling	• The distinction between popular culture and high art • Culture is society is culture
Claude Levi-Strauss	Binary oppositions	• Identities described in terms of opposing ideas
Roland Barthes	Signification	• Construction of meaning in texts
Stuart Hall	Representation	• The process of constructing the identities of social groups by the media
Louis Althusser	Difference Identities	• Classes defined by their differences • Expression of identity through cultural behaviour
Michel Foucault	Discourses – language and meaning	• Languages (codes) used in particular ways to produce selective meanings about their subject
Pierre Bourdieu	Pleasure Participation and appreciation	• Audience enjoyment of consumption • Class differences in cultural consumption
David Morley/Dick Hebdige	Postmodernism	• No certainties in trying to explain media theory (influence) • Form is everything
Jean Baudrillard	Postmodernism	• Media reality and social reality interchangeable
Laura Mulvey	Feminism/gaze	• How we look at the person helps define how we think about them

Bhikhu Parekh (1997) describes five components which define a notion of culture for members of a recognised cultural group:

1 a body of beliefs through which the group members understand themselves and the world, and assign meanings to their social relations and behaviours;
2 values and norms of behaviour which regulate social relations, inform ideas of 'goodness', and are behind key life events such as birth, marriage and death;
3 rituals and expressive arts which communicate collective emotions, experiences and self-understanding;
4 conceptions of a distinctive history and of difference from other groups;
5 cultivation of a common social character (including elements such as motivation and temperament).

KEY CONCEPTS

As a general starting point for this section, it may be useful to refer to the *circuit of culture* described by **Paul Du Gay** et al. (1997), which takes representation, identity, production, consumption and regulation as its key terms (see the diagram). These terms are described below, though not necessarily in this order.

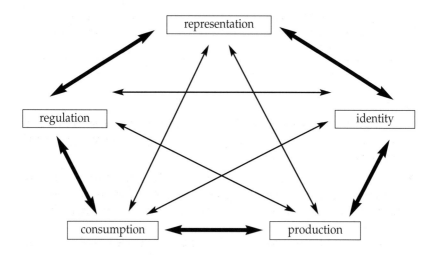

Source: Du Gay et al. 1997.

Difference and correspondence

Difference refers to both social and cultural differences, and to differences between cultural (ie media) products. 'Different from' is what makes for cultural distinctiveness, even identity.

- The idea of difference owes much to the writing of neo-Marxists and structuralists such as **Louis Althusser**, developed in the writing of **Stuart Hall** and of **John Fiske.**
- Negative connotations of difference are to be found within representations of race – the group which is set apart by being represented as different from some norm.
- Positive connotations may be seen when, for example, youth cultures colonise mass-produced artifacts and use them to emphasise the differences of their groups, the distinctiveness of their identities.

Correspondence is about similarities of product, of behaviour, of norms. It is about that which makes a crowd of football supporters a cohesive subcultural whole.

Study point

List three features which make for both cultural similarities and differences between people who may live in widely different parts of the country but who identify with particular teams of groups.

Identity

This concept refers to the sense of self-image and group belonging which is held by members of cultures, and which is itself enhanced by consumption of cultural products and representation through the media.

- Critiques of popular culture are often concerned with identity and class. **Richard Hoggart** was concerned about the 'loss' of English working class culture in the face of mass media production and the cultural imperialism of the USA.
- Fiske celebrates forms of popular culture and the identities they offer for those who consume them – eg wrestling or game shows on television.
- Identity may be in the brand image constructed for a product as well as in the group image constructed by the group's use of that product (among others). The 'cool' component of the identity of a jacket worn by a Hip Hop follower is both part of the specialist company which commercially promotes that identity, and part of the Hip Hop group and its behaviour. Its members borrow, and yet also give it, coolness by wearing it.

- Pessimistic views of identity, generally Marxist, see the media as constructing people as subjects of ideology.
- Optimistic views – post-Marxist or postmodernist – see people as active and in control of their culture, using texts (eg images) and commodities as they want to, and seeing themselves as they want to be seen.

Representation

This concept is more fully discussed in Chapter 6. In terms of popular culture, *representation* is very important in referring to ways in which the media give meaning to cultural groups, construct their identities and assign meanings to the products used by those groups (also promoted through media advertising).

Cultural production

This concept refers to the idea that in an age of mass production, culture is a manufactured thing, or at least uses manufactured products. It may also refer to the fact that ideas about culture are manufactured, through representation. **Theodor Adorno** describes a culture industry which manufactures products for consumption. He criticises the loss of the distinction between high art and low art in this manufacturing process which treats the consumer as the object of its production (Adorno, 1991).

Consumption and commodity fetishism

This concept was formulated by Karl Marx and developed by writers such as Adorno. Cultural products are commodities. Fetishism lies in the values and qualities attached to those products. Marx's concern was that the labour behind the production was 'lost' or concealed: that the goods could acquire a value which had nothing to do with the price of that labour or the cost of production. These concerns are very relevant today. The designer-label phenomenon is a perfect example: a Hilfiger sweater, for example, has an exchange value which justifies a sale price which is not justified by commonsense notions of cost and profit. The sweater stops being just a sweater and becomes a kind of magic object which confers social status upon its wearer. This is just the same as a shaman's magic mask having a cultural value way beyond its materials and labour which made it.

Popular culture is full of such fetishised commodities. The key question raised is whether the value of the product is a 'genuine' cultural creation, or whether it is really imposed on consumers (ie the majority) to the benefit of producers (ie the minority). Marxists take the latter view: ideology in action. Popular culture may be seen as being largely about the consumption of goods – commodities – which also leads one to see social relations as being based on consumption.

Regulation

This concept refers to the mechanisms which modify the distribution and use of cultural products. It leads one back to considerations of what the audience values and wishes to consume – ie to demand. It also leads to reflections on control of production – ie to supply. It leads to consideration of power and control – forms of censorship, and the role of government. Consumption is a kind of social behaviour – eg as with visiting the shopping mall. Consumers (audiences) may choose to visit or not to visit, to buy or not to buy. But they cannot initiate production and supply. They cannot censor or control at source.

Social practices

This concept refers to the social activities and behaviours of a culture, and to the meanings ascribed to those behaviours. The artifacts of popular culture are part of behaviour, and meanings are ascribed to those products. But really it is the activity which is significant. For example, certain makes of skateboard have kinds of value attached to them, financial and social (status, style etc.). But they wouldn't have status without the social practice of skating. Cultural artifacts may indeed conceal social practices. This is true where representation is involved. For example, photographs in magazines of, say, Amazonian tribespeople are likely to present the exotic and different nature of their appearance and environment. What they conceal are the social practices of that people, how they work to survive, how they make friends, and so on.

Ideology and power

In spite of the attempts of some postmodernist criticism to kick the ball of ideology out of court, this term permeates this book and thinking about culture and society. The marketing and promotion of cultural products may be seen as the promotion of the ideology behind those products. In this sense, the person who buys the new car at new registration time is also buying beliefs and values which belong to the interests of those who run things – social status, material wealth, new is good, social competitiveness. These ideological value positions fuel the power of those who produce cultural goods, and pretend to enhance the power of those who consume them. This is an illusion. If that same person (assuming they really needed such transport) had bought a 3-year-old car, it would have made no difference to their ability to transport themselves. But of course commodity culture isn't just about functional necessity.

Signification and production of meaning

This concept is a term from semiotics, and refers to the particular meaning(s) that one takes from the possible meanings within a text. In terms of popular culture, it draws attention to the importance of meaning behind social behaviours and the use of cultural artifacts. For example, bottles of designer lager are artifacts for consumption – the beer literally, the bottle shape and label metaphorically. The choice of the beer, the possession of the bottle, drinking from the bottle and not a glass, all have signification. The consumer is making social meanings about their social position, and about wealth, taste, group identity and (generally) masculinity.

POPULAR CULTURE DEBATES

MASS CULTURE AS POPULAR CULTURE

In this case, the debate is subsumed within a number of propositions:

- Mass production has produced a mass culture which has become popular culture.
- Mass culture has replaced folk culture, which was the true culture of the people.
- Mass culture is dominated by the production and consumption of material goods rather than by the true arts and entertainment of the people.
- The creation of mass culture is driven by the profit motive.

STRUCTURALISTS – CULTURALISTS

This debate could be seen as a difference of opinion between Marxists and postmodernists. In terms of the purpose and outcomes of analysis of popular culture, the argument could be seen as follows:

- The production and consumption of popular culture is underpinned by structures of domination. These structures can and should be sought in the relationship between institutions and in the location of power. Consumers have limited power.

Or:

- Popular culture is about forms of social behaviour and about how items of mass production are used. So if one does want to talk about power, then consumers do have degrees of control over their own culture.
- The assumption of and search for structures is largely illusory because the relationships between institutions are so complex and shifting that determinist explanations of who does what to whom and how are a waste of time.
- The important thing is to look at the meanings and social relations produced by the artifacts and behaviours of popular culture.

HIGH CULTURE (ELITISM) – LOW CULTURE

This debate is one which is essentially bound up with the status of culture in society and its possession by one social group or another. Put crudely, it sets ballet against club dancing, theatre against television, and so on.

- Culture is defined dominantly within the arena of the arts.
- High culture is more valuable than low/popular culture.
- The appreciation of high culture is a sign of personal sensitivity and of social status.

- High culture is an expensive, minority activity, thereby confirming its status.
- Low culture is for the masses and is populist, and is therefore less valuable.

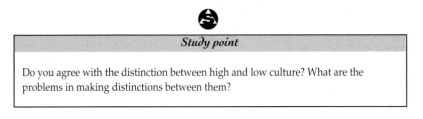

Study point

Do you agree with the distinction between high and low culture? What are the problems in making distinctions between them?

CONSUMPTION AS PLEASURE

This debate is audience-centred and positive in its view of popular culture:

- Consumption is not about mass audiences as passive victims of mass production.
- Individuals and audiences of various sizes achieve pleasure (ie enjoyment) from consuming mass media. This pleasure is a positive thing which the audience has degrees of control over because it actively engages with the text.

THEORISTS ON POPULAR CULTURE

In general, there are distinctions between (classical) Marxist positions on culture, which see it as driven by economic determinants and a top-down class power model, and neo-Marxist positions which are still interested in power structures but see the issue of power being complex, with the culture consumers not simply being victims.

Postwar neo-Marxism also merged with what may be called structuralist critiques of media and culture, which are interested in form and text but which link the meanings drawn from analysis back to a larger model of power and social control. The problem of distinctions becomes the greater when one notes that modernism also embraces structures and organising principles behind the production and transmission of culture. One may as it were be a neo-Marxist and a modernist at the same time.

At least it is clear that postmodernism has rejected the idea of absolute truths about class, power and ideology. On the other hand, postmodernist textual analysis is still concerned with power when it examines how cultural artifacts are used. 'The popular is determined by the forces of domination' because it is 'formed in reaction to them' (Fiske, 1989).

MARXISM

The classical Marxist position is that cultural institutions (ie education) are used by the elite to legitimise its power. Part of that legitimation lies in getting the working class to accept social inequality. Power is exercised through control of the economy and of the means of production. Economic determinants therefore rule social relations and the nature of culture.

It needs to be remembered that Marx lived at a time when the mass media and their kind of cultural production did not exist, though the concept of mass society was embodied in the urban populations of the nineteenth century. Culture was equated with what we would call 'high art'. Popular culture might better be described as folk culture. It was localised, fragmented, generated and maintained by the folk.

Ralph Milliband (1973) summarises a particular view of media (and culture) from a classical Marxist perspective when he reuses a well known phrase of Marx, referring to the media as 'the opium of the people'. Behind this allusion to mass passivity established through mass culture is a continuation of the idea of ideological domination by an elite.

Antoni Gramsci developed ideas about culture and society while imprisoned by the Italian Fascists between 1926 and 1937 (when he died). In many ways, he should be described as a neo- or post-Marxist because his ideas were only published in the 1950s and later, in books such as *Selections from the Prison Notebooks* (1971). He moved away from determinist views of Marxism, but is very concerned with class and conflict. He developed the idea of *hegemony* to describe the means through which one class could maintain control over other classes, by using both *coercive* and *consensual control* to exert power. Consensual control is the most invisible, and is exerted in part, it is argued, through the media and popular culture. Hegemony works when it brings together many cultural elements of society. An example would be the appeal to patriotism through the popular press to justify questionable actions such as the Anglo-American attack on Iraq in December 1998. It could be said that we absorb values through the media, which affect how we behave, and which cause us to behave in ways which preserve the interests of those in power. Continuing to consume would be one of those interests. We not only consume the ideas but also fuel the economy of capitalism by spending our money.

NEO-MARXISM

Postwar (1950s onwards) Marxists reworked what some regarded as simplistic earlier views of class, power and culture. In particular, the notion of ideology and the location of power was developed, for example through the work of Gramsci and the concept of hegemony. The relationships between social institutions and the interplay of power were recognised as being complex. It was no longer believed that the masses were passive recipients of mass-produced culture.

Raymond Williams is extremely important as both a Marxist and a founding father of British cultural studies. *The Long Revolution* (1961) looks at social and cultural change in Britain. It throws over assumptions about the superiority of one kind of cultural expression (high art) as opposed to another. It sees the media and objects of mass production as being part of a revolution. It is interested in the 'meanings and values' in culture, and in how these are changing. **Graeme Turner** (1990) draws out Williams' phrase *structure of feeling*, and its attempt to define the distinctiveness of a given culture. For Williams, culture is society, and vice versa. The meanings about a culture are expressed in forms and acts of communication. So, the media are our culture, and the way we understand, talk about, and respond to the media helps define what our culture is, what it means to us, and what it is that we value about it.

Stuart Hall has been a considerable influence in the development of British cultural studies thinking for over 30 years. Because his positions have shifted and developed with changes in Marxist thought and the growth of cultural studies, it is impossible to summarise his ideas in a few lines. There is a fair summary of his thinking on ideology in Turner (1990). One point that is worth bringing out is his notion of the *manufacture of consent* both by the media and through representations. For Hall, this explains how hegemony works and why the majority accepts the ideology of the minority. This makes the media responsible for social relations and for the production of a culture and cultural attitudes which support the dominant ideology.

Louis Althusser was both a critic of Marxism and a committed Marxist. He is also regarded as a structuralist. His view was that ideology is all-pervasive, that it defines the *identities* which we believe we have as members of a given culture (see Althusser, 1969). This identity is expressed through material practices – what might be called cultural behaviour. So someone who goes clubbing is actually responding to the forces of ideology. These forces work to create our social reality and to maintain class relations. However, he would also say that to be a 'clubber' is to adopt a false identity which conceals the reality of what is really going on, especially in respect of those influences (including the media) which persuade us that clubbing is okay and meaningful.

MODERNISM

It has already been suggested that this term is difficult because it is intertwined with Marxism and because modernist comment on culture stretches over the whole of the twentieth century – so it is hardly modern in the sense of being up to date. Modernist thinking is concerned with rationality and structure. It has often been associated with the arts and with 'high art' at that, rather than with that messy amorphous thing called popular culture. So it is easy to see modernism in the pared-down building of Corbusier or the intellectualised music of Stockhausen. But these examples go back 80 odd years. Modernist thinking about society and culture was driven by reflection on the consequences of urbanisation, industrialisation and mechanisation. It sought (like Marx indeed) to adduce certainties about social structures and relationships, to see the big picture, and to achieve idealised models of how things ought to be. For a critical cutting edge, one would have to include philosophers and Marxists under the umbrella of modernism, which as a term does not immediately conjure up a repertoire of critical concepts so much as a set of attitudes.

Walter Benjamin (1936) refers to the significance of mechanical reproduction. He was talking about the camera and the cultural production of images. The power of technology to duplicate sounds and pictures through various media has irrevocably changed the nature of culture. Images have become cheap and widely available. The ability to communicate evidence of our world and versions of our world has produced knowledge, though some would say not understanding.

Richard Hoggart (1958) provides an important critique of mass culture. What is interesting is that he faces in two directions at once. He writes sensitively about the value of the working class culture in which he was brought up, and is certainly an early 'culturalist', an inspiration for cultural studies. But he also preaches the value of high culture and talks contemptuously about the youth culture of the 1950s. What he did do was use literary forms of *textual analysis* in commenting on the culture which he did admire, including popular songs.

INTERACTIONISM

This is concerned with the nature and significance of interactions between people, and between people and the media. It is possible to look at the relations between people who make media, eg at how the producers of drama make the kind of cultural artifacts that they do. Or one could take the example of how the presence of TV news cameras sometimes encourages delinquent behaviour.

Max Weber refers to intentionality, control and meaning when he refers to actions by and between people. These actions are part of our cultural behaviour, and we have to use our cultural knowledge to make sense of them, of our own social practices. He talks of *action relevant to meaning*. Weber gave space to the influence of individuals over society, unlike Marx. He was not so convinced of the importance of class, though he was interested in the sources and exercise of power.

Stan Cohen famously examined interactionism and cultural behaviour in his study of Mods and Rockers in the early 1960s. This is examined in more detail elsewhere in this book. He looked at the interaction between the youth groups, between local people and the groups, and between the media and those groups. He concluded that media accounts of supposedly anti-social behaviour by the young were much exaggerated, and that the media were guilty of creating a false sense of alarm among the public – *moral panics*.

FUNCTIONALISM

This view of society is interested in the relations between social institutions, but is not (like Marxism) critical of unequal power relations. In terms of popular culture, one would be interested in those institutions which embrace that culture. This could refer to the relationship between the media and the family. Functionalists would argue that the family may have had to change in response to the media, which have become a part of their domestic experience and entertainment.

Emile Durkheim conceived of those institutions in terms of an equilibrium between them. Social processes would move to repair any imbalance and to restore order, though by adapting and changing. Society itself creates collective representations – generally held views on issues and behaviours – which inform the nature of balance and change.

So, changes in popular culture would be seen as a response to changes in the media, and vice versa.

STRUCTURALISM

This assumes the existence of structures or organising principles behind cultural behaviours and within cultural artifacts. It came out of the examination of tribal rituals and stories, and has been extended into the organising principles of narratives in general. Structuralism is allied with semiotics, and so the signs within a text are taken to be organised in a meaningful way, according to some principles. This has led to the analysis of images in particular, and of how meanings are encoded within them and then decoded by the viewer. These meanings may themselves be seen as relating to conditions of social inequality and to the exertion of power (Marxism).

Claude Levi-Strauss was a social anthropologist who was also interested in language. There were key debates about whether the structures that rule language are generated deductively by children or whether they are born with deep structures in the brain which help them make sense of the language being used around them. This notion of structures both behind and within cultural material interested Levi-Strauss, and was applied by him to understanding tribal stories and rituals. In particular, he deduced oppositional structures – *binary oppositions* – within this cultural material (Levi-Strauss, 1963). This idea about how cultures make meanings also relates conveniently to discourses. In this case, it is easy to see opposed ideas between the discourses of male and female, which help to explain differing representations of gender in popular culture texts.

Roland Barthes (1957) also developed ideas from linguistics and through semiotics. His structured approach to the organisation and meanings of signs offered a methodical way of dealing with media texts.

POSTMODERNISM

This has reacted against the notion of certainties and structures. Postmodernism is all about the study of popular cultural forms. It is about the study of form as much as content. It is about the connections between texts (*intertextuality*). It believes that the media have come to define and dominate social relations, even to define what we understand reality to be. Postmodern texts play with style and form, are not interested in logical narrative structures or moral conclusions. They make distinctions between high art and low art meaningless by plundering high culture for humour and for references. They relish the use of irony in terms of black humour and of cross-referencing texts.

Postmodernism cut in somewhere in the 1980s as a reaction against modernist certainties. It celebrates popular culture. It reflects on the nature of pleasure in texts and on what audiences do with texts. It is not interested in Marxist agonising about the location of power within some structured relationship between great social institutions. At the same time, postmodernists may still discuss the nature of power and of social relations.

David Morley (1996) provides a neat account of postmodernism being defined in opposition to modernism:

- a rejection of total solutions: there are no absolute truths or 'answers' in modern society and culture;
- a rejection of teleology, or certainties about how society works: there are no perfect models of how things work 'under the surface': all we can be sure about is that surface itself – ie style and appearances;
- a rejection of idealism, of Utopia: there is no ideal society or perfect culture.

Michel Foucault has been particularly interested in the notion of discourses. In this case, he argues that all our ideas are framed by discourses, by ways of thinking about a given subject. He separates discourse from ideology – others argue that this does not make sense. He is saying that the way we think about some aspect of our culture – madness was a particular example – creates its own truth about that subject. So it was at one time that people believed that men were 'naturally' more reasonable than women. The language and ideas of the gender discourses asserted this truth, and so it was true. But discourses and their meanings shift. This is a kind of relativism about the truth of cultural experience which is different from the determinism of the Marxist. It also ties in with the postmodernist idea that what media culture says is reality becomes reality.

Pierre Bourdieu (1984) is much referred to by John Fiske in his useful book *Understanding Popular Culture* (Fiske, 1989). One of Bourdieu's most interesting ideas broadly distinguishes between working class (popular) culture and middle class (highbrow) culture in terms of involvement and detachment, the difference between *participation* and *appreciation*.

Jean Baudrillard argues against the view that there is some absolute cultural and social reality that exists outside what we see and read through the media. His view is that this media reality has become continuous with social reality. What is in the screen is as much part of reality as what we do in our everyday lives. He is taken up with intertextuality, with a view that every sign has some kind of relationship with every other sign. In Baudrillard's world, says **Kenneth Thompson** (1997), 'reality disintegrates into images and spectacles.'

FEMINISM

Feminism is involved with the study of representations, with the meanings in texts, with the nature of audience consumption, and with social relations, but always with reference to how and why gender matters. It has a necessary connection with Marxism because it is also concerned with the expression of power within gender, as gender operates within popular culture. Feminists would be concerned with whether popular cultural texts replicate inequalities of power in relations between men and women. It can be said that feminism is about using existing critical tools in the particular area of gender.

Laura Mulvey (1975) exemplifies an influential piece of analysis which concentrates on *text* and *pleasure*. In discussing the nature of *the look* (ie how the viewer is brought to look at the film), Mulvey argues that film storytelling is organised to allow men to look at women for pleasure, but not vice versa. So the cultural artifact reveals social inequalities which are based on gender and notions of *patriarchy*.

Angela McRobbie embraces postmodernism in her interest in text, style and consumption. She argues for the continued study of the nature of pleasure and identity. She talks about changing modes of feminity (see also the chapter on youth culture). She refers to changes in female identity in which sexuality and assertiveness co-exist in media representations and in young female behaviour. Popular culture, in terms of magazines or of raves, embodies and expresses social change.

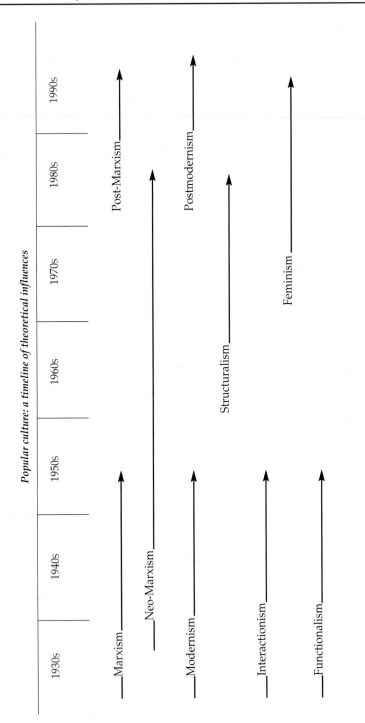

Popular culture: a timeline of theoretical influences

	1930s	1940s	1950s	1960s	1970s	1980s	1990s

Marxism

Neo-Marxism

Modernism

Interactionism

Functionalism

Structuralism

Feminism

Post-Marxism

Postmodernism

SUMMARY

Popular culture is defined by beliefs and values, by behaviours and rituals, and by a sense of history and of distinctiveness – all shared by a given social group.

Key concepts in popular culture include the following:

- a sense of difference and of identity
- how identities are represented
- how culture is produced
- ways in which culture and social relations are equated with goods
- how meanings about culture are produced within texts
- how ideology operates within cultural goods and practices.

Key debates about popular culture include the following:

- in what ways mass culture and popular culture are one and the same thing
- in what ways popular culture is an expression either of forces of domination or of people's autonomy
- the differences between high culture and low culture, and their significance
- the Americanisation of mass culture
- pleasure in consumption of mass culture
- the loss of identity through mass popular culture.

Key theories about popular culture come through the following:

- versions of Marxism which are all concerned with the exertion of power through cultural institutions;
- modernism, which is concerned with the rethinking of form and structure but which wants to preserve high art values apart from popular culture;
- interactionism, which is interested in people as much as in institutions, and in how this interaction helps make sense of popular culture;
- functionalism, which sees the media as contributing to the tendency of social institutions to seek a state of balance (not necessarily of power);
- structuralism, which reads structures, and meanings about these, in cultural behaviours and artifacts;
- postmodernism, which rejects structures and bypasses ideology in favour of text, form and meaning, all within a positive view of the power of popular culture;
- feminism, which sees popular culture as being essentially bound up with meanings about gender and inequality.

STUDY GUIDES

Group work

1 Contrast and compare the display of identity by one youth group in terms of **John Fornas'** three definitions of youth (see p 118).
2 Discuss and map out the 'complexities' and 'fluidity' of a chosen youth group's identity.

It is suggested that you first collate the display and behaviour signs of identity in that group. Then chart the appearance of these signs in other examples of youth groups or subcultures.

Practice Questions

1 To what extent is the emergence of youth cultures a reflection of other changes in society?
2 Does the representation of youth by the media support a view of the media as an agency of social control?

Coursework suggestions

1 Research the idea of commodification in relation to teenage girls as a subculture. Ethnographic methods and analysis of cultural products are likely to yield ideas about how far girls become a cultural phenomenon by being consumers.
2 Use semiotic analysis and other appropriate methods to examine contrasts between the different ways in which a given youth culture represents itself, and the way that it is represented in the media.

You may come across similarities or differences of meaning about the youth group. You may be able to explain these differences in terms of ideology, discourse, hegemony and notions of power incorporated within those concepts.

4

MASS MEDIA: INSTITUTIONS AND POWER

Introduction

THIS CHAPTER IS about:

- the nature of media ownership
- the implications of this for media products and for the effects of these products on society
- issues raised by media patterns of ownership
- critical perspectives on media and power
- constraints on that power
- major theories about mass media and society.

OVERVIEW: SOME MAJOR ISSUES

It can be argued that there are a number of consequences of and issues arising from the nature of media ownership in Britain. This section is a development of topics announced in the introduction, but also acts as an agenda for the rest of this chapter.

Table 6: *Theorists, concepts, key phrases and propositions in this chapter*

THEORISTS	CONCEPTS KEY PHRASES	PROPOSITIONS
James Curran and Jean Seaton	Pluralism Determinism	• Choice and social pressures negate media power • Media power is exerted in collusion with a 'ruling class'
R Negrine	Power and control	• Institutional control of resources is moderated by market forces (audience demand)
Dennis McQuail	Location of power	• This may variously be within institutions, society, individuals, audiences

- *Global power.* Ownership of the media crosses countries and continents: the operations and interests of Reed-Elsevier, for example, span Holland, Britain and America; and interaction with society (the audience) needs to take in this global dimension.

A key issue here is how this power can be (or even needs to be) moderated when it is partly outside the control of national governments.

- *Government and media interdependence.* The expansion of channels of media communication has increased the means through which government can communicate with society and social groups. The media have become essential in the processes of elections and of government publicity. Equally, the broadcast media depend on government for their licences to operate, and all news operations depend on government as a major source of stories: people like Alastair Campbell, the Prime Minister's Press Secretary, have operated both as journalists and as spin doctors for the Prime Minister.

A key issue here is how far this relationship has become corrupting and against the interests of individuals and social groups.

- *The rise of marketing.* Media operations have become dominated by the marketplace: media products and audiences are marketed as commodities, and the media depend on advertising for their income (but see later remarks about the BBC on p 49).

A key issue here is how far the media have become creatures of market forces and should or should not be allowed to continue to operate as such.

- *The manufacture of lifestyles.* It is not only advertising which operates through constructing its audiences in terms of their lifestyles: all media businesses (like manufacturers) see their consumers in terms of niche markets and social groups with certain kinds of lifestyle.

A key issue here is that of the influence which media have on the social behaviours and preferences of groups within society, especially youth groups.

- *A portfolio of products.* Media companies are no longer concerned largely with one business, as they were up to about 50 years ago. Then, the old-style press barons were only interests in newspapers, and the Hollywood moguls were still in charge of a film business. Now, the new media corporations have interlocking patterns of ownership across various media businesses. This means that they make their money (and have their influence) through a range of media.

A key issue here is simply that of the power that this gives them to have a voice which talks with the different tongues of newspapers, radio and television (as is the case with the Daily Mail & General Trust Group which owns the *Daily Mail*, half of Teletext and one quarter of GWR radio).

- *The dominance of genres.* The products of media organisation are shaped by the notion that they should fall into categories. These categories or **genres** – eg quiz shows, a *Lethal Weapon* movie, the romantic novel – work in the interests of producers by giving them an easy formula to work to and a focus for marketing. However, the degree of repetition of material may not work in the interests of the audiences concerned.

A key issue here is that the dominance of genre material leads to a dominance of the ideologies within that material, as well as to suppression of original untypical work.

Activity

Working in a group, investigate the following three aspects of a possible relationship, based on given genres, between institution and audiences:

1 the frequency of a given type of material
2 the ideas within the material
3 the audience response to the material.

It is suggested that you take the topic of romance and investigate it through either romantic novels or romantic magazines.

In the case of 1, you could investigate the existence (and proportions) of a recognisable category of romance through library and newsagents' shelves, and through listings for TV and films.

In the case of 2, you could use textual analysis approaches to uncover what is said about romance and how it is treated in some examples of the genre.

In the case of 3, you could use focus group interviews to investigate what attracts the audience to reading such material.

Table 7: *Dominant media ownership and titles*					
NEWSPAPERS					
MIRROR GROUP	ASSOCIATED NEWSPAPERS	NEWSCORP	UNITED NEWS & MEDIA/MAI	HOLLINGER	GUARDIAN
Daily Mirror *Sunday Mirror* *People* *Independent*	*Daily Mail* *Mail on Sunday*	*Sun* *News of the World* *Sunday Times*	*Daily Express* *Sunday Express* *Daily Star*	*Telegraph* *Sunday Telegraph*	*Guardian* *Observer*
TELEVISION					
GRANADA	CARLTON		UNITED NEWS & MEDIA/MAI		
LWT Yorkshire Tyne Tees	Central Meridian Anglia C5 GMTV		HTV Meridian Anglia C5		
CINEMA					
SONY	MATSUSHITA	NEWSCORP	TIME/WARNER /TURNER	VIACOM	DISNEY
Columbia Tristar Touchstone	MCA/ Universal	Fox Searchlight	Warner Bros	Paramount	Disney Miramax
BOOKS					
PEARSON	THOMPSON	NEWSCORP	RANDOM HOUSE	HOLTSBRINCK	REED
Longman Penguin Signet	Nelson	HarperCollins Unwin Hyman	Arrow Jonathan Cape Chatto & Windus	Macmillan Pan Picador	Methuen Heinemann Octopus
MUSIC					
SONY	MATSUSHITA	EMI	TIME./WARNER	POLYGRAM (PHILLIPS)	BMG MUSIC (BERTELSMANN)
CBS	MCA	Chrysalis Virgin		Island A & M	RCA

MEDIA INSTITUTIONS: PATTERNS OF OWNERSHIP

The media demonstrate repeated characteristics in the ways that they are set up and run. The significance of these patterns has to do with what is rather loosely called the power of the media. Media ownership has developed, with the effects of:

- increasing the scale of operations
- increasing the range of control
- increasing the volume of resources available, both technical and financial
- increasing the volume and range of products
- decreasing the number of competitors.

VERTICAL INTEGRATION

Media companies try to control all aspects of their operations, usually summarised as production, distribution and retailing (or exhibition for cinema). So, Warners makes and markets films and owns cinemas.

CONGLOMERATION AND DIVERSIFICATION

Media take a stake in other media. They diversify into other businesses, and they themselves are bought up by larger corporations. Universal Pictures is owned by MCA. MCA is owned by the Japanese Matsushita corporation. Matsushita owns many other companies having nothing to do with the media.

INTERNATIONALISATION

The three processes above take place across countries and continents. So, International Thompson, for example, is Canadian. It owns Thomas Nelson publishers in Britain. It owns the high street firm Thompsons Travel. It also owns many other publishing and financial services on both sides of the Atlantic (such as the *Jane's Guides*).

COOPERATION

Media companies will cooperate, to share costs or to ensure dominance of a given marketplace. Co-production is common in film and television. Commercial television production is dominated by Carlton (Central), Granada (Yorkshire, London Weekend) and Meridian (Anglia), who cooperate in sharing out products with the small companies. British film distribution is dominated by the American majors, with whom cinema owners like Virgin have to cooperate. It has been argued that some of these examples of cooperation, mainly carving up the distribution of products, could be breaking laws against cartels – ie major companies conspiring to carve up a market against the interests of consumers and competitors.

COMMERCIAL/PUBLIC SERVICE MODELS OF CONTROL

British media are dominated by a commercial model of ownership in which the essential purpose is to compete and to make money. Emap is an example of a successful company which has bought into local newspapers and found profitable niche markets for specialist magazines. This company might argue that it is fulfilling a public service by satisfying demand. But this of course equates demand with expenditure: ie assumes a large enough readership spending enough money to make it worth publishing. Small or poor audiences get left out.

Table 8: *Emap PLC: selected media holdings*

NEWSPAPERS – 76 regional, including:	MAGAZINES – 237, including:
Bedfordshire Times	*Smash Hits*
Suffolk Free Press	*More*
Norfolk Citizen	*Q*
Yorkshire Coast Leader	*Elle* (agreement with Hachette to
Milton Keynes Citizen	publish in Britain)
The Mercury Series	*Parents*
Newmarket Journal	*Sky*
	PC Review
	Looks
	New Woman
	Slimming Magazine
RADIO	OTHER
Radio City Ltd (50)	Maclean Hunter publishing
Piccadilly Radio (50)	Four printing companies
Cardiff Broadcasting (50)	Frontline (distribution) (60)
Metro Radio Group	Choice Publications (50)
Emap Radio	
Red Rose Radio	
West Yorkshire Broadcasting	
Gwent Area Broadcasting	
Kiss FM Radio	

EMAP OWNS THESE BUSINESSES OUTRIGHT, EXCEPT WHERE INDICATED BY A FIGURE (%) IN BRACKETS. ADAPTED FROM WILLIAMS, 1996.

The great *public service model* in our culture is the BBC, funded by a licence fee and with a remit to provide education and information and to serve minority interests. However, new management and the Conservative government in the 1980s has firmly pushed the BBC into the marketplace, where it behaves like a commercial enterprise even though it has no shareholders. Equally, Channel 4, which is also required to serve minority interests, though funded by its advertising spot profits, has arguably done a good job with its 'alternative' programming. In any case, commercial television is moderated by the ITC, which runs the transmission system, awards the business contracts to the likes of Anglia and vets advertising and programming. It ensures a degree of social responsibility. So, public service models of the media are in a sense forced on television and radio. Other media, whatever the constraints on them (see below), don't work to a public service model, though they may still claim that they serve the public.

PRODUCTION AND DISTRIBUTION

Whether or not vertical integration has taken place in a given media organisation, still the overall pattern is one of concentration of ownership in areas of production and distribution. So, W H Smith and Surridge Dawson dominate the distribution of newspapers and magazines in Britain. WHS is also a major retailer of these products. Companies like EMI, Warners, Sony and Polygram dominate the production of CDs. Successful independent producers tend to get taken over by the majors: Island Records was bought by Polygram in 1990.

The apparent diversity of product titles or company names is in fact an illusion. Pearsons owns Longmans, and Longmans owns 10 book publishers, including Penguin books.

Study point

1 Make a list of examples, across the media, of public service uses of media that you know of. Examples might include traffic information on radio or listings magazines.
2 In what respects may the funding of media influence their ability to act as a public service?
3 Make a grid representation of points for and against an interactionist view of the relationship of media with audience.

INSTITUTIONS, POWER AND CONTROL

Often, it is assumed that media power resides directly or indirectly in the media institutions, the owners and the producers. However, if one takes a process view of interaction between media and audience, then power may be exercised at many points of that process:

1 Does power reside in the media owner or in the market forces which that owner 'has to obey'?
2 Is power really exercised by the producer (or perhaps the editor) rather than the owner/chairperson/board of directors?
3 Should we be talking about the power of the text, the building of influence into the media material?
4 Is there at least some power vested in the audience? There is the power not to buy, or even the power to resist ideas, as with Hall's 'oppositional readings' by audiences in which the audience does not take on the meanings that the text clearly expects them to.

Table 9: *Media groups: market share*					
GROUP	DAILY PAPER	MARKET SHARE (CIRCULATION)	SUNDAY PAPER	MARKET SHARE (CIRCULATION)	BROADCAST INTERESTS
News Corp	*Sun* *Times* *Today* (folded Nov. 1985)	35.6%	*News of the World* *Sunday Times*	38.2%	40% of Sky
Mirror Group	*Mirror* *Record* 43% *Independent*	23.8%	*Sunday Mirror* *People* 43% *Independent on Sunday*	31.1%	20% of Scottish TV Wire TV and Live TV (cable)
United Newspapers	*Express* *Star*	13.8%	*Sunday Express*	9.2%	
Daily Mail & Group Trust	*Mail* *Evening* *Standard*	14.8%	*Mail on Sunday*	12.2%	20% of West Country TV Channel 1 (cable) Stakes in various radio stations
Hollinger	59% *Telegraph*	7.3%	59% *Sunday Telegraph*	4.2%	
Guardian Media Group	*Guardian*	2.7%	*Observer*	3.1%	15% of GMTV
Pearson	*Financial Times*	2.0%			14% of Sky
Carlton					Central TV, Carlton TV, 20% GMTV, 36% ITN 29% Meridian
Granada					Granada TV, LWT, 11% Sky, 36% ITN, 20% GMTV, Yorkshire– Tyne Tees TV

Source: The *Financial Times* 23 May 1995.

Curran and Seaton (1997) suggest that there are two traditions to be taken account of:

1 the **pluralist** view, which argues that the great variety of social pressures on the audience means that the media cannot have a significant effect on that audience;
2 the **determinist** view, which argues that they can, and that it is the relationship of the media with the governing class which is most significant in this respect.

They argue that there is 'as yet, no adequate vocabulary to describe the relationships between the media, individuals and society'.

Ralph Negrine (1996) says cautiously (with reference to the press) that 'it is probable that ownership does contain within it the potential for direct and indirect control.' He points out that proprietors do appoint editors and do allocate resources. There are particular examples of owners like the late Robert Maxwell directly interfering in the content of *The Mirror*. However, Negrine would say that examples like this are too occasional and generalised to construct a theory of influence. He points out that whatever newspaper owners believe, in the end they will go along with the 'laws' of the marketplace – anything to sell copies.

McQuail (1983) suggests that there are three main questions about media power:

1 the effectiveness of the media as an instrument for achieving given power ends;
2 the question of whose power interests are exercised (those of class or society or individuals?);
3 do the media increase, sustain or diminish existing inequalities of power in society?

He argues that the evidence is that within considerable limits, the media do have some power to achieve some effects. He also suggests that for a variety of reasons (by action or omission) the media do 'protect or advance the interests of those with greater economic or political power in their own societies'.

Study point

1 What do you think are the 'great variety of social pressures on the audience' (see the pluralist views on p 67) which mean that the media cannot be a dominant influence on the audience?
2 What 'inequalities of power in society' (see McQuail above) are there which could be affected by the media?

EXPRESSIONS OF POWER

Power has different ways in which it is exercised. Describing features of the expression of power helps identify how influence may occur, though this still leaves large questions about the quantitive and qualitative nature of media effects.

- *Repetition of material.* In the first place, media products may achieve power through sheer repetition of material (and therefore of ideas). This point ties in with genres – repeated types of media material. For example, the *Lethal Weapon* cycle of films reinforces through repetition, ideas about masculinity and the male buddie relationship.
- *Cultural production.* Media institutions have expressed their power through becoming producers and shapers of culture. They are as much a social institution as school or family. Children sing advertising jingles in the playground; families go to a multiplex cinema for a night out; groups of mates go to the pub for a few beers and the football match on the bar TV. In this sense, culture is not something which exists in society, with the media then latching onto it and doing something with it. Sky TV sport is as much a cultural experience as going to the live events is – they are different in the activity but the same in principle.

Max Horkheimer and Theodor Adorno (1972) use the phrase *cultural industry* to describe the creation and distribution of cultural goods. They see it as replacing live, local or subcultural activity. But evidence does not support this negative view. Media cultural production exists alongside 'live' cultural activities. Magazines about new kinds of dance music appear because of what is happening live in the clubs. The screening of sports on TV demonstrably increases live participation in them.

- *Cultural imperialism.* This phrase proposes that Western media institutions, notably those of America, are creating a new kind of empire of ideas across the globe (Tunstall, 1978). But this idea about how media power is exerted is now being questioned. Certainly, there is no argument about the economic reach of media corporations – the power of the Hollywood distribution system reaches literally into every major city on the planet. Also, it would be foolish to suggest that the ideological positions built into TV texts which are exported around the world, will have no effect at all on their audiences. But it is being pointed out that specific cultural conditions of reception in different countries make it difficult to go along with a simple 'exercise of power' model. **Annabelle Sreberny-Mohammadi** (1996) asserts that

the international media environment is far more complex than that suggested by the 'cultural imperialism' model whose depiction of a hegemonic pied piper leading the global media mice appears frozen in the realities of the 1970s.

She points out that Brazil exports programmes to 128 countries, including Hispanic channels in America. Cultural exports don't only come from America and Europe.

- *Allocative* and *operational control*. These are the notions developed by Adorno and others that media institutions may express their power through two different kinds of control. One is about the power to allocate resources to certain kinds of product. This clearly relates back to the locus of power in financial resources and to the power of media owners. The other is that exercised over the workings of the media institution, ie operational detail as opposed to policy. In this case, one would be talking about control exercised by the marketing manager for a magazine, by the circulation manager of a newspaper, or by the editor of the day for television news.

Activity

Investigate the proposition that the media are encouraging or suppressing cultural activity in the area where you live. Research a range of activities.

Identify the nature of the activity, eg line dancing or clubbing, or being a *Hollyoaks* fan. Deal with questions such as:

1   Does the activity seem to be more passive than active?
2   Does it involve the mass media in any way?
3   Does it have any other distinguishing features?

What conclusions regarding the proposition could you draw from the range of evidence?

HIDDEN POWER

The phrase *false consciousness* has come out of the Frankfurt School of Marxism. The idea is that the media express their power by creating a false idea about social relations and values, so that what we think we know to be true is a delusion – a view of the world much constructed through the media.

There are three key terms which help explain hidden power in media, society and culture. All of them have been developed through Marxist analysis of power and of social relations.

1 Ideology
(See also Chapter 2, p 18.) This term describes a coherent set of ideas and values expressing a view of the world (social, economic and political), how it is and how it should be. It also stands for ideas about power relations in society, who has what sort of power, who does not, who should have power, who should not.

As a concept, it has been reworked and interpreted by those coming from a variety of disciplines, including sociology and philosophy. It has become common to talk about a dominant ideology, or a dominant view of the key values in a social structure – values which benefit those who run society. 'The ideas of the ruling class are in every age the ruling ideas ...' (Marx). Ideology permeates all our talk, all our communication, all media. The meanings that we may get from analysis of media texts are bound to be ideological. What precisely those meanings are – what it is to be a child, for example – is a matter for some argument.

Points of evaluation

1 Critiques such as those of Ralph Milliband would argue that we accept social inequalities because ideology operates as a means of social control. It may be added that ideology is expressed through forms of entertainment as much as through forms of information-giving. This gives ideology a 'voice'. This voice endorses the inequalities of a class system not least because it proceeds from a kind of media ownership that is capitalist and conservative. It is conservative because media owners are an elite group in society and have a privileged position to conserve. This uncompromising view of ideology and its workings has not room for notions of pluralism or free choice (see the section on pluralism on pp 67–8 below).

2 Other writers such as Stuart Hall see a more complex situation in which some media material may indeed have a kind of neutrality and even an ability to reflect on the very ideology which it is meant to be a 'victim' of. But, talking particularly of news and current affairs broadcasting, Hall would say that *some* detachment may create the illusion that a much greater detachment is at work, when in fact it is not.

2 Hegemony

This is about the ways in which the invisible power of ideology is exercised. It is about the processes by which one set of ideas belonging to one social group become dominant in a society. It may be about processes in which there is a struggle for dominance between social groups. The term comes from the work of Gramsci who, broadly speaking, saw this struggle as a class struggle, and one that had much to do with culture. In discussing the concept, one could talk about the middle class colonisation of football, symbolised by Nick Hornby's novel *Fever Pitch*. One class tries to gain hegemony over another with reference to football, which itself is only in the public arena because of its presentation in the media.

3 Discourses

- These are sets of meanings about a great range of 'topics'. These meanings are produced by the ways that language is used and understood. 'Language' could mean any form of communication, including the visual language of photographs, television and cinema. The idea is that the way we 'talk' about something says everything about the way we think about it.

The word 'topic' is used loosely here to try to explain the huge range of discourses which are in our heads, which are in the way we talk with one another, and which are in the ways that the media talks to us. So, there are gender discourses about being male or female; institutional discourses about education or medicine; and media discourses about television in general or news in particular.

- From Althusser's point of view, education might be an example of an ideological state apparatus, which ensures that those who run things stay in control. At the same time, there is a discourse of education whose meanings are locked into words we use about it: teacher (not adviser); pupil (not learner); education authority (not support services). These words are about status, hierarchy and power. They are about how we think about education. They explain why adults have been known to go weak at the knees when returning to school as parents!

- It is also argued that discourses reveal power struggles between different sections of society. The languages used by youth cultures are not only part of their identity, they are also a way in which those social groups can say 'we are resisting the values of the dominant culture.'

- The term discourse was first developed by Michel Foucault. Edward Said uses the idea in talking about 'Orientalism' – the discourse of, our views of, the way we talk about, things oriental. This discourse has its origins in the way that Western nations sought to assert their power over countries of the East in the days of empire (and to diminish the status of those countries and their inhabitants). You can see the workings of this discourse in the representation of oriental villains in films and novels, or in the ways that the Iraqis were depicted in news reporting of the Gulf War. You have only to play a word-association game starting with 'Chinese' or 'Arab' to understand the power of discourse, the meanings produced by selective use of languages.

The media and aspects of power

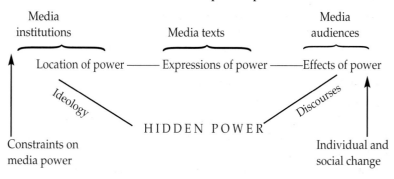

Media power is located within institutions and their operations, is expressed through the exercise of kinds of control and through texts, and reveals its effects in terms of audience attitudes and behaviour. As a hidden force, it is exercised through the working of discourses, and is shaped by ideology.

Activity

Investigate the discourse of family and representations of families by carrying out the following activities. You are advised to work with at least one other person.

1   Ask at least 10 people to give word associations (comprising about 10 words or phrases) around the idea of family.
    a   What words are common in the last two sets of answers?
    b   What words are positive or negative in the last two sets of answers?
2   List as many types of family or household unit as you can.
    a   How do the words fit with the family types?
    b   What dominant view of family is projected by the words, and how does this relate to the family types?
    c   What view is denied?
    d   Who gains from the dominant view?

What do the results of this investigation tell you about how ideology works?

CONSTRAINTS ON MEDIA INSTITUTIONS

The discussion so far of the nature and extent of media power might suggest the inevitability of effects and the implacability of that power. Neither of these things can be shown to be true.

CENSORSHIP

Censorship implies direct interference by an arm of government, usually in respect of programmes or printed content. The nearest thing we have to such a body is the Broadcasting Standards Council (1988), set up by the government, which inspects video, film and TV material. The media in Britain are not censored as such except in times of national emergency – eg the Falklands War in 1983. However, the above Council does not look at everything, and its judgements are not legally binding on the media.

Generally, British media are self-censoring, through bodies such as the Advertising Standards Authority, the Press Council, The British Board of Film Certification, the BBC governors, and the Independent Television Commission

(ITC). The operation of these bodies is to be understood in the context of official and unofficial links with government. There are frequent public debates about how effective these bodies are, often in relation to:

1 violence and sex in content
2 news intrusiveness and payment for stories
3 political interference.

Examples of these respective points are:

1 the debate about David Cronenberg's film *Crash* whose theme is the relationship between sexual excitement and death/suffering in road crashes. The debate ranged between exponents of the 'gratuitous violence' school and advocates of the film's critique of society's love affair with speed and the car;
2 the argument about news coverage of the late Diana, Princess of Wales, fuelled by such photographs as those of her working out in a gym, and climaxing in assertions about the paparazzi being partially responsible for her death in a car accident;
3 the debate in late 1998 about political party spin doctors attempting to manipulate news reporting. British Prime Minister Tony Blair had a meeting with the Italian media magnate Silvio Berlusconi. Blair's press secretary attempted to deny that the meeting had occurred in the first place, and then sought to play down the discussion of media interests and ownership of satellite channels.

OTHER CONSTRAINTS

Legal constraints

Examples of these would be the laws against libel and slander, which restrain media from publishing or broadcasting anything they like. The Prevention of Terrorism Act 1974 enters the political arena and prevents media from producing material that would either encourage terrorism or hinder authorities in their pursuit of terrorists. In practice, the news media nearly always cooperate with the police of the Home Office if asked to back off a story on such grounds, so that the restraining force of the law is not tested. Likewise, laws relating to discrimination and to trades description constrain media (especially advertising) from producing anything which is demonstrably untrue about goods for sale, or which encourages discrimination on grounds of gender or of race.

The Official Secrets Act 1989 is also political in the sense that it is used to restrain the media from investigating or reporting on activities of government departments. But, for example, in the 'arms for Iraq' affair in 1992, judges declared that matters which the government wished to keep secret about the exporting of arms to a 'hostile' country could not be suppressed under the Act.

Material constraints

Essentially this is about the limits of the resources which the media have available for production and distribution. These resources would be mainly money, technology and time. A budget of £200,000 for an hour of quality TV drama sounds generous, but it offers limitations when compared with the £10 million spent on an hour of the average Hollywood film. We are used to the notion that the world is the newsmaker's oyster. But, apart from political objections to Western news teams entering certain countries, there are still many countries which do not have the ground-station satellite technology which we assume is universal.

Political constraints

In the sense that government brings in laws, it could be argued that all legal constraints are also political. However, there is a distinction between the examples above which affect the operation of the media, and those, such as the Broadcasting Acts or Wireless and Telegraphy Acts, which explicitly license, describe and restrain the setting up of broadcasting companies – radio, television, cable, satellite. Pirate radio is by definition illegal and unlicensed, regardless of whether it fulfils a social need. The BBC is established by a Royal Charter. Commercial broadcasting is by permission of acts of Parliament and the licenses granted by the ITC – which the government also sets up.

The government provides the media with materials for their news operations. The broadcast media also know that the government has the power to control their activities – for example, it is Parliament which sets the base figure for the BBC licence fee (which is index linked), and therefore its income. Parliament has also placed a special tax on commercial TV broadcasting (the Levy). But equally, the government *depends* on the media as a means of publicity for its policies, and as an arena for political debate and the conduct of elections.

Study points

1 What are the different ratings for films in Britain, and what do they mean?
2 What protections for children are there with regard to television, newspapers and the Internet?
3 Why are there differences between the various media in terms of the ways in which they self-censor material for children?
4 What do the answers to questions 1 to 3 above say about:
   a   views of children as a group within society
   b   assumptions about the media?

THEORIES ABOUT MASS MEDIA AND SOCIETY

Ideas about how one may describe the nature of mass media and their relationship to society and social groups may be cross-referred with those theories and concepts described in Chapters 2 and 3. These descriptive theories themselves focus on particular ideas such as social order, social control, free choice, cultural production and economic determinism.

McQuail (1996) proposes a distinction between theories about what he called the *social domain* and those about the *cultural domain*.

In terms of media performance and the social domain, he sees two aspects. One is the media acting as an agency of social control upon society. The other is media representing and promoting social solidarity by both recognising differences between social groups and showing the advantage of cooperation, for example.

In terms of the cultural domain, he would see social control as being about the endorsement of dominant cultural activities. Social solidarity is shown when alternative subcultures are recognised and accommodated.

FUNCTIONALIST THEORY

This view of media sees them as performing some sort of job, serving a function, for society or the state or even the dominant ideology. The problem is that one will have a different view of what media functions should be or appear to be, according to where one is coming from. So the audience might see media as serving different purposes from those that media owners see themselves as serving.

McQuail (1983) argues for five categories in describing media purposes for society. He sees the categories as remaining the same when one looks at different interest groups' views of functions, even if those groups interpret the categories slightly differently. A summary version of his view would read as follows:

1 *Information*: to provide information about events and conditions in society, and about relations of power;
2 *Correlation*: to interpret this information, to support authority and norms, to build consensus;
3 *Continuity*: to express the dominant culture and new cultural development, to maintain common values;
4 *Entertainment*: to provide amusement and diversion, to reduce social tension;
5 *Mobilisation*: to mobilise opinion and action in support of common social objectives relating to areas such as work or economic development.

It should be recognised that sometimes media initiate these functions, eg the *Independent on Sunday* campaigning for the legalisation of cannabis. Sometimes, they are used by other institutions, eg Amnesty International advertising its cause through newspapers.

Strinati (1995) argues that 'the basic problem with functionalist explanations is that they account for the causes of social phenomena in terms of their consequences.' In other words, what the media seem to do now for society explains why they emerged in the first place. But, for example, radio did not emerge only with the function of providing entertainment, at the beginning of this century. Initially, it was as much a two-way as a broadcast medium, and it was used by the British navy to coordinate its battle fleets.

So, Strinati sees functionalist interpretations as being too simplistic and flawed. 'Functionalist arguments often suggest ... the eternally guaranteed continuation of the system which the institution is supposed to serve.' Because the media mobilise opinion, they serve a purpose which ensures that they must always be there to fulfil that purpose.

PLURALIST THEORY

Such views of media and society generally argue that many media offer a wide range of material for a range of audiences. These views do not see a real problem with the idea of media power. They would argue:

- that people are not faced with a coherent, controlling view from institutions;
- that audiences do have real choices over what they read and watch;
- that the range of social influences on audiences is such that it is impossible to talk about the over-riding influence of the media.

Pluralist views of power originate in the work of Max Weber. He argued for democratic representation through a range of political parties. These parties, and separate pressure groups, would represent the interests of different sections of society.

Points of evaluation

1 It is of course true that parties and pressure groups have their views represented through the media.
2 They may also advertise their views.
3 There is an underlying notion that everyone has a voice, everyone has a choice. This is not true. Media are not plural to the extent that they represent all social sections. Not all sections are represented equally. Having money ensures that one has a louder voice than others. Some voices are suppressed or ignored.

LIBERTARIAN (LIBERAL PLURALIST) THEORY

Libertarianism is in a sense the child of capitalism – the belief that a free-for-all will work out for everyone in the end. A free market in ideas freely published gives free choice to society. In particular, it is argued that this freedom gives the media the scope for acting as a watchdog on government, checking on how well government serves society at large. In this sense, the media would also act as representatives of the public, as well as a source of public information.

Liberal pluralism is the view (or ideology) taken about the media by most people working in the media. It argues that a free market brings a free press and free media. The problem is that there isn't a free market. One's ability to start a newspaper is determined by having enough cash, as Eddie Shah found out in 1983 when he started the *Today* newspaper and then ran out of money a few years later and had to sell up. Nor is one free to say what one likes in a newspaper, even as a reporter or an editor.

In terms of effects on society, such pluralists argue that the media cannot have much influence.

Points of evaluation

Boyd-Barrett (1995) summarises a distinction between (liberal) pluralism and neo-Marxism with regard to portrayals of violence in the media. He suggests that:

1 the pluralist is interested in whether the individual may be made to become more aggressive;
2 the Marxist is interested in whether the individual is caused to become more compliant with the forces of law and order;
3 from the libertarian viewpoint, it is true that the media played a part in setting out the 'cash for questions' row in the early 1990s, when a few MPs were exposed as having become the tools of lobbyists. But they signally failed to challenge the British government in the early 1980s when it led the country into a war with Argentina and without (on the basis of early opinion polls) the clear support of a majority in the country.

SOCIAL RESPONSIBILITY

This theory is a reworking of libertarianism to suggest that media should temper the free-for-all with a sense of responsibility for the greater social good. It is also high minded in principle but short in evidence in practice. When a young black man, Stephen Lawrence, was murdered on a London street in 1993, in general the media did not act as watchdogs with responsibility for asking questions about police failings in handling the case. It is the parents and supporters who have finally caused those questions to be asked through using the process of law.

McQuail (1983) describes the idea as one where 'media ownership and control is to be viewed as a kind of public stewardship'.

MARXIST THEORY

Marxist positions on the relationship of media with society run counter to pluralist views. They may be described as control theories. However, dogmatic Marxist assertions of the indisputably malign controlling classist influence of the media upon society are no more satisfactory than vague unfounded pluralist assertions about a wonderful world of freedom and choice.

What is clear is that any Marxist view argues that the media mainly represent conservative positions on social issues, and represent the values and interests of those who have power in society, generally denying a voice to those who do not have power. From this point of view, media exercise some sort of control over society. In particular, they control, to a degree at least, people's view of what society is like and should be like – *false consciousness*. The media promote consumerism among the audiences because this is in the interests of owners who run the businesses to make money.

So, society is seen as being in a client and subservient relationship to the media. These media, through representations for example, maintain in society inequalities of wealth, power and privilege.

Graham Murdock and Peter Golding take this view – what Strinati calls *the political economy perspective.*

• They assert that the nature of ownership does matter because it does give the media power, and that this power is exerted against the interests of certain sections of society.
• They pick up on economic determinism in suggesting that economic forces have led to the concentration of ownership which has emphasised the kinds of control which media do have over society in the production of ideas about social relations.

Points of evaluation
Conflict theory, as a development of Marxism, is related to the concept of hegemony (also see above, p 58).

1 In this case, it focuses on class conflict as underlying social struggles for power.
2 It can be argued that the media are involved in that struggle if they privilege the views of one class and deny the interests of others. For example, news reports on 'New Age Travellers' mainly report them in negative terms and support the actions of authorities in trying to move them on or trying to make them law abiding. The Travellers consequently feel they are being oppressed and denied natural freedoms.
3 Strinati (1995) also criticises conflict theory for 'a form of class reductionism whereby all culture is explained by its relation to class struggle'. He argues that 'the distinctively Marxist emphasis on economic determinism is sociologically limited.' In other words, Marxism is not the only tool for understanding media culture and how this affects the audience.

FEMINIST THEORY

Feminist perspectives on media and society are interested in how the media construct views of women, and why. They are interested in the implications for socialisation by gender.

Liesbet Van Zoonen (1994) distinguishes between *radical feminism* and *socialist feminism*. Radical feminism takes a kind of Marxist position on what the media institutions do to women and to ideas about women. In particular, it sees the media as being an expression of patriarchal oppression which has to be exposed and resisted. Socialist feminism takes a less uncompromising line in using a more complex Marxist position which includes analysis of class and economic factors, as well as approaches to ideology (as already discussed above). But still the power which creates an unequal position for women in society is seen as being located in media institutions.

Points of evaluation

1 Cultural approaches to feminist study are prepared to take a broader view of the problem of power for women and where it is located.
2 They would not simply blame male-dominated institutions but would, for example, look at power in a social context and power in other social institutions.

POSTMODERNIST THEORY

Postmodernism is difficult to get a handle on not least because it rejects what might be seen as modernist attempts to find some certainties: describing organising principles in texts (structuralism); describing coherent principles in the relationship between media and society (determinism). These principles have been called *metanarratives* – one example would be Marxism and its attempts to 'tell a story' about social relations which makes sense of everything. Postmodernism says these metanarratives don't work.

The interests and characteristics of postmodernism are easier to describe:

• the idea that media material is simply part of our reality and not 'something else';
• the intertextuality of films like *Natural Born Killers*, in which references to other films are part of understanding it;
• the use of irony in telling stories, especially black humour;
• the splintering of narrative/editing, as in the film *Pulp Fiction*, against the conventions of the average realist text;
• playing with realism and surrealism;
• the idea that there is no distinction between art and popular culture: definitions of high culture/low culture are no longer meaningful.

Points of evaluation

1 Postmodernism is saying that media culture is reality for the audience.
2 The audience embraces this culture and does not have to be a victim of it.
3 Postmodernism is more interested in the pleasures of the text than in its possible effects on society.

SUMMARY

There are a number of issues which arise from the nature of media ownership, not least those which question whether this ownership is in the interests of a free society or in the interests of groups within society.

Ownership is characterised by the expansion of control – over aspects of the one media business, and into other media businesses.

This control, especially when concentrated in the hands of few and fewer owners, is bound up with consequences for the power of media. This power is located in control of resources, of production, of distribution, of products, of ideas within those products. The power of ideas may in effect be hidden and be described in terms of ideology, hegemony and discourses. These ideas may influence social relations, social behaviours and social attitudes.

Media Theories: focus of interest

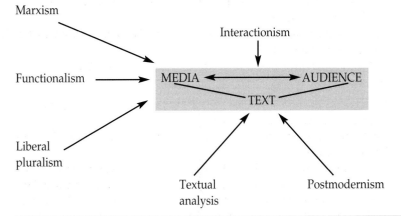

Dominant theories about the media have tended to look at institutions and to be concerned with what the media do to people.

Elaborations of these theories (interactionism) tend to see institution, text and audience as being equally important.

Structuralist approaches (see 'Textual analysis') and postmodernism tend to be more interested in text and style, and less convinced about institution's ability to affect audiences.

The media are constrained by law, by their relationship with government, and by their own voluntary controls.

Media institutions operate in particular through routines, on the basis of marketing strategies and the needs of the marketplace, and under the influence of self-created notions of professionalism.

There are a range of theories about the relationship between media and society. Generally, these polarise into a contrast between versions of libertarianism and versions of Marxism: between ideas about the media as working freely within a free society, and media as a controlling, shaping force of society.

STUDY GUIDES

Group work

1 Investigate a local media institution (eg newspaper or broadcaster), using interviews, their promotion material and other sources you can locate. Deal with three main questions:
  a To what extent does this business fit in with the patterns of ownership described in this book?
  b Which local audiences benefit from your case example's output?
  c Which local groups apparently do not benefit?

  What conclusions can you draw about the interests of media businesses compared with the interests of audiences?
2 Discuss the implications of the 'new media' – cable, satellite, digital TV – for ideas about media power.
3 Examine a range of material in at least three examples each from the tabloid and the quality press. Use that range, and an analysis of the treatment of lead articles, to discuss support for liberal-pluralist (ie choice) and Marxist (ie control) views of the press. You might express your findings in a grid format, using these two views. The vertical, liberal-pluralist axis would include categories referring to the range of material (or lack of), the range of views (or similarity of), and the uses and effects of headlines and photographs. These categories should help you focus on the idea that genuine pluralism should provide a range of views on news items, as well as a range of news for different audiences; whereas a controlling press will offer little real choice, and will treat news as a market commodity and as a way of endorsing dominant views of society.

1 How far do controls and constraints on the media work in the interests of individuals and groups within society?
2 Explain how ideology works through the media to maintain social inequalities.
3 'Gender and power ... form the constituents of feminist theory.' (Van Zoonen, 1994.) How may feminist theory connect with the study of media institutions and their power?

1 Research ideas about what functions the media may perform for society and for different social groups. Correlate these functions with examples of specific media texts.
   Take a specific text and evaluate what functions it seeks to perform, and in whose interests (eg *Crimewatch* from TV).
2 Investigate the notion of Public Service Broadcasting (PSB), as described in the terms of reference by which the BBC and Channel 4 operate.
   a Do the accounts of responsibilities and programming requirements look similar or different for each channel?
   b Does the notion of PSB revealed actually seem to serve a wide range of social groups?
   c Do the differences in funding between the channels seem to matter, in terms of this idea of public service?
3 Investigate the idea of 'consensual control' as this may be exerted through the media, specifically through material for young children. You may find it useful to address the following questions:
   a What kinds of ideas or views of good and bad behaviour are put across?
   b How are they put across in an attractive and entertaining way?
   c Who benefits from these ideas?

5

MEDIA PRODUCTION AND NEWS

Introduction

THIS CHAPTER IS about:

- critical views of media production in general
- three key aspects of media production: imperatives, practices and context
- critiques of news production, and some key concepts here
- key concepts relating to the manufacture of news and its meanings
- the presentation of news, its construction of meanings, and the issue of bias
- a case study in news: the Gulf War on television.

SOME CRITICAL VIEWS OF MEDIA PRODUCTION IN GENERAL

In general, commentary on media production assumes that it is part of a *process*. This process may be described with reference to the business of production or to the sequence of events which culminates in audience reception. What the media produce for society has often been described in terms of *goods*, *culture* and *meanings*. These three terms may be associated with the concepts of *commodification*, *culture and social practices*, and *ideology*.

1 What comes out of media production, programmes or books may be described as 'goods': these goods are *commodities*, objects for sale – even the ideas within a magazine could be seen as commodities. So, the relationship between media and audience becomes part of economic activity: production links to consumption.

Table 10: *Theorists, concepts, key phrases and propositions in this chapter*		
THEORISTS	CONCEPTS KEY PHRASES	PROPOSITIONS
Stan Cohen	Deviancy	• The presentation of selected groups as abnormal or criminal to some degree
Stan Cohen/ Stuart Hall	Moral panics	• The exaggeration by bad news stories about the behaviour of given social groups
John Galtung and Mari Ruge	News values	• Newsmakers' criteria for selecting stories
James Curran and Jean Seaton	Pluralism Determinism	• As producing choice of news • As producing lack of choice
Michael Schudson	Social construction of reality	• A selective view of the world, of society, of social reality
Greg Philo (GUMG)	Consensus	• The idea that there must always be a compromise solution to conflicts raised in news – so consensus is an ideological position
John Hartley	Discourse	• News has its own language and meanings, and incorporates other discourses

2 Another idea is that *the media are making culture*: they help create cultural experiences which become part of our social practices or activities. For example, the genre of chat shows – *The Jerry Springer Show* et al. – are separate cultural goods and yet are mixed up with people's lives and conversations. Or again, some young men both practise Saturday night 'laddism' and experience it as part of media culture in items such as drinks adverts. In fact, it would be argued that there is no clear division between culture in the media and culture as practised in life.

3 The third notion is that *media production is about making meanings*: about our lives, our beliefs, our relationships and so on. It is argued that ideological beliefs about social relations and power are the same thing as those meanings. The production process cannot help producing ideology (but not necessarily reproducing it absolutely, for ever and ever).

Stuart Hall (1994) uses a model which refers to the relationship between producer and audience as being a fractured one. There is *encoding and decoding of meaning*. But what the audience reads into the text may not be the same as what the producer thought they had inscribed in the text. The meaning structures shown in the diagram below will be different for producer and audience. He argues that the meaning is produced as much at the point when the newspaper is read, as at the point when it is written. He calls them 'differentiated moments within the totality formed by the social relations of the communicative process as a whole'. For example, if one took a news story about a politician having an affair, then a newspaper might structure this in terms of the consequences for the politician's career or for their party. But the reader might structure it within a moral framework of condemnation, or within notions about politicians and their behaviour, without any interest in the political implications. Although this chapter concentrates on production, this cannot easily be separated from the reception of products, and from ideas about audience. Making comics or disks or films is part of a process of communication which operates within a social context.

Encoding and decoding: production as process

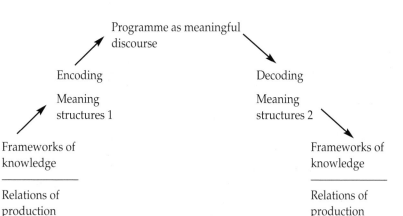

Producers and audience as part of one process but encoding and decoding meanings on the basis of different structures.

SOURCE: HALL, IN GRADDOL AND BARRAT, 1994.

David Morley (Seiter et al. (ed) 1991) makes critical references to the application of the 'classical' Marxist economist model to media production, which is also seen as the production of mass culture. Morley is still within the area of process when he says that 'production is only brought to fruition in the spheres of circulation and exchange.' In other words, production only means something if you also talk about distribution, text and audience response. In referring to audience, he does comment (as do many others) on the notion of consumption. One is still here in the area of Marxist thinking – ie regarding the idea that media manufacture goods which are consumed by viewers and readers.

John Fiske (also Seiter et al. (ed) 1991) refers to this same notion when he says that 'television is a cultural commodity.' 'A programme is a commodity produced and then sold to distributors.' He also argues that the way that we pay for TV means that we do have some choice about what we consume within available programming.

Study points

1   Produce a diagram which shows the stages in production for a CD or a newspaper, and which refers to the kind of selection of material which goes on at each stage.
2   Give three examples of social activities which are linked in some way to media materials.
3   Take one example of a category of media material (eg sitcoms) and explain what ideas about social relations are produced within it, and how.

THREE ASPECTS OF MEDIA PRODUCTION

1 PRODUCTION IMPERATIVES

The media are businesses. Production is a collaborative process, using the skills of many people. This may not exclude creativity as an impulse and shaping force behind production. But this factor does suggest that the romantic notion of the inspired artist producing work which in some way improves the lives of those who read or see it, is largely a false idea. For the media and society, social and economic relations are intertwined. Imperatives behind media production are:

- *the need to recoup investment*: when the newspaper industry invested millions in new compositing and production technology from the late 1980s onwards, it then needed to produce papers which sold;
- *the force of competition*: whether one is dealing with the rising audience numbers in multiplex cinemas or the generally static numbers of newspaper

readers, there is a pressure to compete or else lose business. Rupert Murdoch has been bringing down the cover price of *The Times* for years now, to a point where it can hardly be breaking even. Competition and offers wars between the tabloids are a common experiences for readers;

- *the pressure to hold or increase audience (or readership) figures*: the essential measure of success in media – and a reason why workers keep or lose jobs – is feedback on audience consumption. Whether it is ratings for radio listeners or circulation figures for a magazine, production (including the style and content of the product) is affected by this pressure;
- *the slot to be filled*: production is driven by existing commitments. A newspaper cannot go out with blank pages. Broadcast channels have to be filled with something. Whether the need to fill space by given deadlines actually benefits the audience in any way, is debatable.

These production imperatives all relate to the idea that the media operate in a marketplace. It is the demands of that marketplace which drive that production.

2 PRODUCTION PRACTICES

There are common practices across the media which have implications for what is produced, how it is produced and how it may affect the audience.

- *Genre* material dominates in decisions about commissioning production, because its familiarity makes it attractive to the audience, easily marketed and cost effective in the mechanics of the production process.
- *Production routines* appear across the media, most obviously with genre material. Given the complexities (ie involving numbers of people and technology) involved in much media production, it is attractive to be able to develop habitual ways of manufacturing and presenting material, even if this may lead to repetition of treatment and indeed of meanings for the audience.
- *Media interaction* is a common feature of contemporary production, not least because it may mean sharing costs, or extending the range of marketing. The cost of films are commonly shared between more than one production company/distributor. Books such as *The Horse Whisperer* increase their sales by association with the successful film made from the book.
- *Marketing* (as already mentioned) has become a production practice in that promoting the magazine or the programme has become part and parcel of making it. The audience is the object of competing attentions. The relationship between audience and text is inevitably changed by the marketing which prioritises some meanings about the text above others.

3 THE PRODUCTION CONTEXT

Media production practices operate in a certain kind of commercial environment. The marketplace is part of that environment, which shapes how and why products such as programmes are made and directed at given audiences. But more than that, there are other factors which affect how media institutions operate:

- *polarisation* of, for example, newspapers or CDs into mass markets and specialist markets. This is based on the principle that one can either make a lot of money by selling huge numbers of a product – eg about 3 million copies of *The Mirror* every day – or target a product at a relatively wealthy audience whom the advertisers will pay good rates to reach. People become Classic FM listeners or *Telegraph* readers in a reformulation of social groups;
- *niche markets*: finding small specialist audiences by recognising both social change and changing patterns of consumption. Successful publishers such as Emap have consciously sought specialist markets in music and teenage magazines, for example;
- *rising costs*: in general, media production goes on getting more expensive, though not consistently and rarely at a rate which the market won't bear. So, the average cost of making a film has doubled since 1970. Newsprint for making newspapers goes on getting more expensive. The pressure is for media companies to find ways of making more money to compensate – selling spin-offs like soundtrack albums with films – or to find ways of reducing costs elsewhere – eg newspapers bringing in new technology so that they can sack workers and reduce the wages bill;
- *increased competition*: the expansion in the numbers of media channels (broadcasting and publishing) means that appealing to the audience becomes all-important. What this 'appeal' actually means in terms of quality of product is much debated, with strong arguments accusing the media of dumbing down.

Activity
Investigate and produce a case study of a media product in terms of production imperatives *or* production practices *or* production context. You may find it useful to refer to a book such as Du Gay et al., 1997. Explain how different aspects of the production area chosen affect how your product comes to have the kind of form or treatment that it does have.

NEWS AND MEDIA THEORY

John Fiske (1982) says that news 'enjoys a privileged and prestigious position in our culture's hierarchy of values'.

NEWS AND CRITIQUES OF MEDIA

James Curran (1996) discusses news and its possible influence in relation to general theories of the media. If one takes these to fall into two broad camps –

pluralist and free choice, and determinist and about shaping society – then his views are as follows:

• Neither position is sustainable in relation to news production and to news reading by audiences.
• He points out that 'different social groups have unequal access to the media.' So there is no state of free plural access (let alone plurality of views).
• He also criticises determinist views expressed in Hall's phrase as 'the hegemony of the powerful'. Curran points out that the powerful 'are not all of one mind, and the rest are not always excluded.'

John Hartley (1982) is clearly influenced by Marxist critiques of the media, but is mainly interested in news as text and as meaning. All the same, he is well aware of other areas of criticism of the news as a part of mass media:

• 'News comes to us as the pre-existing **discourse** of an impersonal social institution which is also an industry.'
• In his emphasis on the use of discourse analysis, he points out that 'in discourses, language systems and social conditions meet.' The way that news uses words and visuals to talk about social conditions, social behaviours, social groups and social conflict, constructs meanings about these four factors. Those meanings are then taken on – though not necessarily uncritically – by the news audience.
• Hartley argues that however one may describe news operations and the ways that we understand news products, we still have to take account of the bigger picture. News 'has meaning only in relation to other institutions and discourses operating at the same time'. Indeed, he is also aware that there are specifically sociological dimensions to constructing a critique of news – the social organisation of news institutions or the social function of the news.

The following are two concepts which have already been explained in relation to the media in general but which are now applied to the news in particular.

NEWS AS COMMODITY

News material is indeed a commodity because it is bought and sold via news agencies. There is a price on news stories. *Stringers* (freelance journalists) are paid for stories which they uncover (or create?!) and which are used. Television broadcast news editors exchange news stories at 10 am every day, for cash. The fact that news is a commodity means that it is no different from any other media 'goods' – scripts that are paid for, programmes that are bought by other countries.

Social relations become commodities when they too have a price on them. People are paid money for the news stories, perhaps about a notorious family member as in the Fred West murder case in the early 1990s – their relationship acquire a cash value.

Market information about social groups and their disposable income is also bought and sold – there is a price on the economic relationships between social groups. This information will, for example, help determine the advertising rates set around the main evening news slots.

So, the idea of commodity – and the influence of the marketplace – is all-pervading.

NEWS AND IDEOLOGY

It may be argued that if the media as an institution communicates ideology to its audiences, then news as a particular operation within the media is an especially potent carrier of this ideology. This is because news is supposed to fall within something called fact, as opposed to fiction. It is because the subject matter of news is political activity, economic events and social behaviour. News cannot help reporting on the exercise of power, and it is hardly surprising that it takes positions (albeit concealed ones) on that power. Generally speaking, it endorses ideas like the rule of law through the judiciary, the natural primacy of the family as a social unit, and definitions of terrorists as expressed by the government.

It is when one looks at the few examples of alternative news practices that the force of ideology becomes apparent.

- The *Undercurrents* alternative news organisation has no access to broadcast channels, even though its material is not exactly designed to bring down the state.
- It distributes 'other' news via video tapes.
- Its subject matter is typified by items of protest and criticism of the operations of large institutions – the abuse of power.
- Its news items openly privilege the views of 'protestors' rather than those of authority. It is prepared to turn items into mini documentaries, being free from the confines of the news slot. Its approach reminds one of how ritualised news practices are – and that there are other ways of doing things.
- Its positions on its subject matter show how ideologically conservative mainstream news is.

Study points

1   Make a list of points explaining why different social groups might have 'unequal access to the media'.

2   Set up parallel lists under two headings, 'Present' and 'Absent'. Under 'Present', write down the categories of people that you believe are likely to appear in newspaper stories. Under 'Absent', write down those categories that are unlikely to appear. What may one conclude about news and ideology from these lists?

NEWSMAKING

News is a manufactured thing, as much as any other media product. The notion that it is dug out of the mines of truth is false, though this would be an attractive metaphor for journalists who lay emphasis on 'getting the real story' and 'getting the facts straight'. The subsections which follow refer to the structures and social conditions of that manufacturing process.

NEWS PRODUCTION

This is a collaborative process in which the team is held together by the authority of the editor, by a shared sense of values and by an understanding of roles within the team. Press editors are sensitive to the attitudes of their proprietors, to competition for scoops over other papers, and to the views of their readership. Broadcast editors of the day have similar sensibilities, even though it is a head of news division, not an owner, to whom they are answerable. So, news is produced within a framework of views, of working practices, of a group of people.

Michael Schudson (1996), in referring to newsmakers' objections to phrases such as 'the social construction of reality' defends the sociologist's position by saying: 'we did not say that journalists fake the news, we said journalists make the news'.

He also draws attention to studies which demonstrate the interdependence of journalists and dominant institutions (see comments on media and government in Chapter 3). As he puts it: 'the story of journalism, on a day to day basis, is the story of the interaction of reports and bureaucrats.'

Schlesinger (1978) argues that the newsmakers themselves are bureaucrats:

- 'the doings of the world are tamed to meet the needs of a production system in many respects bureaucratically organised';
- Newsmaking is referred to as a system 'operating with a determinate set of routines'.

NEWS AND PROFESSIONALISM

Schudson, in the article cited above, discusses research which indicates how professionalism is tied up with the systematisation of news production, and with the validation of news values which drive the selection and shaping of news materials.

Gaye Tuchman (1978), as referred to by Schudson, describes news in terms of 'pertinent information gathered by professionally validated methods'. The problem is that the professional methods and values become self-fulfilling. This is the way that we do it because this is the way that we have done it.

Schlesinger describes this problem when referring to subeditors whose career progress was endangered when they disagreed with the news judgement of the editor. Expressed in this way, professionalism becomes protectionism.

NEWS FLOW: NEWS SELECTION

Newsmaking is a process which flows from the first contact with the source of the news through to the time that it appears on the page or on the screen.

However, one can distinguish here between the three stages of:

1 gathering and selection
2 editing (further selection)
3 construction.

This is broadly about what happens before material arrives in the newsroom, and about what happens once it is there. In both these stages, one can see that the news 'event' flows through gatekeepers who may allow or disallow, shape or leave, the material which passes through their hands. Examples of these gatekeepers might be a foreign correspondent who picks up a story from a stringer in the field, or a copytaster who samples and evaluates copy flowing into the newsroom. Newsmaking is very much a production-line business.

News is also often not new:

- Stories run for days.
- Coverage of stories is planned in advance.
- Stories are borrowed from other news sources.

Broadcast editors always read early morning newspapers with an eye to their later bulletins. All editorial floors are tapped into the Press Association, and can buy material from that agency. Government press conferences are regularly covered by the big newsmakers. Indeed, all socially accredited sources such as the police, the CBI and the unions are regularly covered and are a major source of news and comment on news issues. Because these institutional sources have status and credibility, it follows that the news also acquires authority and credibility by using them.

NEWS VALUES

The selective process of news gathering and editing is fundamentally driven by newsmakers' assumptions about what subject matter and treatment is valuable and what is not. This value might be expressed in terms of importance to society. But it could also be seen as a measure of ideological importance. It raises the question: valuable to whom, and why? And yet the sense of news values (ie newsworthiness) is so assimilated into the professional thinking of newsmakers that they have been surprised to have such questions raised. Their response to questions about what is chosen for the news, and why, is a circular one: it is a matter of 'professional judgement'. The origin, expression and consequences of those judgements are not questioned.

It is not hard to deduce news values through:

- content analysis of news material – repetition and frequency speak for themselves;
- newsroom sources which have confirmed, in research, that if one has pictures with which to present a story, then that story is more likely to appear than an item which lacks visuals;
- analysis of presence and absence – a story about royalty and disaster will appear, where a story about an ordinary person and happiness will not.

There have been many descriptions of news values, of which probably the most well known are the definitions compiled by **John Galtung** and **Mari Ruge** (1970) (see Table 14).

The notion of influence behind the potential impact of news values may be described in terms of *social reproduction* – the perpetuation not merely of ideological positions and social values, but also of social differences.

Table 11: *Newsworthiness/news values, after Galtung and Ruge, 1970*	
Frequency	The event must begin and end within the publication cycle of the news organisation reporting it
Threshold	The event must pass a certain size threshold to quality for sufficient importance to be newsworthy
Clarity	It must be relatively clear what has actually happened
Cultural proximity	It must be meaningful to the audience of the news organisation in question
Consonance	The event must be in accordance with the framework of understanding which typifies the culture of the potential audience
Unexpectedness	Within the framework of meaningfulness under cultural proximity and consonance, the event must be unexpected or rare
Continuity	If an event has already been in the news, there is a good chance it will stay there
Composition	Coverage of events is partially dictated by the internal structure of news-gathering organisations
Actions of the elite	Events involving elite people or organisations are more likely to be covered than those of unimportant people
Personification	Events that can be seen in terms of individual people rather than abstractions are more likely to be covered
Negativity	Bad events are more newsworthy than good ones

SOURCE: ADAPTED FROM BRIGGS, A. AND COBLEY, P. (ED), 1998.

One might consider how stories involving ethnic minorities are covered. Are such social groups present or absent in most news? If they are present, how are they represented, positively or negatively?

NEWS AGENDA

The idea of news setting an agenda of stories for public consumption is related to values. Items will appear on the agenda precisely because they are valued. The agenda may be identified through approaches such as content analysis which measures the prominence of news stories in terms of the space or time given to them. Influence is explained in terms of the priority given to certain news stories becoming the sense of priority then acquired by the public. What the news says is important becomes important. An extension of this argument is that the priorities set by dominant institutions (particularly the government) are taken on through news-gathering practices. So, the government influences media and thus the audience.

Activity

Examine and compare the main stories in at least two each of the quality and the tabloid press. Identify the types of stories (see the 'News agenda' section above) and the apparent reasons for their being selected (see the 'News values' section above).

1   What are the similarities and differences between the quality and tabloid examples?
2   What is suggested about social differences and about the different readers as social groups?

NEWS PRESENTATION

This area is taken to be about form as well as about content. The style and devices of presentation raise questions about:

- the objectivity of news
- its representation of social reality
- its influence on the audience in terms of constructing that social reality.

From one point of view, the fact that there are a number of daily newspapers and an increasing number of news programmes and channels in broadcasting, suggests two things:

1 that there are different versions of the news for different audiences;
2 that the news cannot purport to be 'the truth' because there are so many truths out there.

NEWS PRESENTERS

The role of news presenters is peculiar to broadcasting, where the person behind the desk – but only heard on radio – becomes the *narrator* of the news programme. They are storytellers in the sense that they tell us the main plot and introduce other 'characters' in the story. The presentation of press news cannot be discussed in this way. There are a few columnists of character, with individual voices. Newspapers do have a kind of house style, with degrees of formality and informality.

Fiske (1987) comments that 'news works through stories that make sense of reality in just the same way as fictional stories.' He argues that events and issues are personalised, that people who appear in the news become characters within its narrative: 'Social and political issues are only reported if they can be embodied in an individual ... social origins of events are lost ... '

The audience forms a kind of relationship with the newscaster as personality, as they become assimilated into the former's social reality. Our sense of what the news is, is bound up with how we evaluate the news presenters. News controllers are well aware of this. So it is that the presenters are designed through their manner and appearance to signify the *authority* and *truthfulness* of news.

THE CONSENSUS MYTH

One ideological position which is at the centre of the way that broadcast news is handled is the notion of *consensus*.

In *Bad News* (1982), the Glasgow University Media Group talks about 'an ideological perspective which is founded on the view of consensus, "one nation" and "the community" ... '. This is also about the idea that political and social issues can always be resolved through agreement – that there is a middle ground for agreement, and that one is unreasonable not to seek this. Such agreement may seem to be all very well in that it will work for peace, stability, law and order – it will favour social control. But then whose peace and law and order is being endorsed?

Points of evaluation

1 A consensus solution to a public workers' pay dispute – perhaps involving nurses – sounds attractive. But it may be that an agreement (which the news

machine would certainly talk up) actually ends up leaving nurses still poorly paid. The point is that it is the *idea* of agreement which dominates. So does the idea that official bodies for mediating agreements will produce a fair solution.

2 Those who criticise the mechanism for reaching agreement, let alone the nature of the agreement itself, are presented as being unreasonable. As Hartley puts it (1982), 'in the consensual model, there are no dissidents.'

3 Ideology, working through the news, whitewashes over contradictions and conflict between those who run things and those who disagree.

MORAL PANICS

This aspect of news presentation recognises that newsmakers place items on their agenda by selectively talking up some event and then turning it into a kind of social crisis.

Hall et al. (1978) examined news treatment of young black muggers and the rash of stories about mugging incidents. It was demonstrated that the numbers of such attacks was exaggerated, and that the notion that the elderly were frequent victims was simply untrue: other black people were more likely to be victims.

Cohen (1987) describes moral panics as a kind of reaction against 'folk devils', against perceived threats to society – 'a condition, episode, person or group of persons emerges to become defined as a threat to societal values and interests'. News takes it on itself to speak for society. Yet society is not cohesive, of one mind. So one asks whose interests are being defended when a moral panic is generated. This is not to suggest that news stories of this type are always untrue, or that there are no social issues to be discussed. But it is the treatment of the topic and the profile that it is given – usually only for a few weeks – which is a distortion.

In the 1980s, stories about an Aids epidemic ballooned in news coverage. In the process, inaccuracies and mythologies about Aids being a gay disease and about how Aids is passed on were developed and retold. Gay people were demonised in the process of making this story. Some newspapers suggested that an epidemic, of even a pandemic, was about to break and eventually kill a significant number of people. With due respect to those who *have* died, this has not happened.

DEVIANCY AND NORMS

It is suggested that moral panics are often about sections of society who are branded implicitly as deviants, as being 'not normal'. The media, and news operations in particular, are a significant part of that 'branding' because they communicate it publicly. They represent social groups in a negative way.

Hall (1978) suggests that labelling in news (see the diagram on page 92) is part of the process of representing groups and their behaviour as deviant. People who are called 'hooligans' or 'terrorists' are positioned differently from those who might be called 'protesters'.

This process of branding groups and behaviours is in effect a process of **social control**. Writers like Foucault have investigated ways in which treatments and definitions of madness and sanity have been used as a mechanism of control, as a definition of normality and abnormality. The government of the former Soviet Union was notorious for branding dissidents as mad and actually putting them into mental institutions.

BINARY OPPOSITIONS

Analysis of media material has drawn on principles of structuralism and narrative analysis. One form which emerges is a structure of opposing ideas or characters or backgrounds, which are more or less explicit in the story. So we all understand the notion of heroes and villains, or the struggle between good and evil.

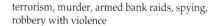

Deviancy and the consensual model: social boundaries

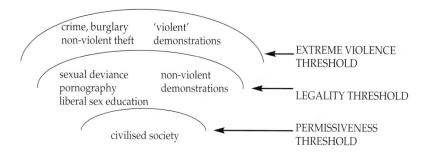

SOURCE: HALL ET AL., 1978.

News can be seen in this way. Deviants or criminals are opposed to law-abiding citizens and the police. The audience for news is in effect invited to see people around them in these terms. News stories are indeed constructed in terms of conflict between individuals: issues are personalised so that they may be understood in this oppositional way.

Chibnall (1977) sees these oppositions in terms of two sets of values which are described as legitimate or illegitimate (see Table 15). They are based on his analysis of crime reporting in the British press. He sees them as values which inform newsmakers' evaluation and presentation of events. This would in turn inform newspaper readers' understanding of these events. It is ironic that ideology appears as a negative value, given that the list clearly represents an account of ideology itself, of 'common sense' values which are taken for granted.

BIAS AND IMPARTIALITY

Debates about bias in news and the impartiality of news are at the heart of critiques of newsmaking for several reasons.

Table 12: *Binary oppositions in news values*	
POSITIVE LEGITIMATING VALUES	NEGATIVE ILLEGITIMATE VALUES
Legality	Illegality
Moderation	Extremism
Compromise	Dogmatism
Co-operation	Confrontation
Order	Chaos
Peacefulness	Violence
Tolerance	Intolerance
Constructiveness	Destructiveness
Openness	Secrecy
Honesty	Corruption
Realism	Ideology
Rationality	Irrationality
Impartiality	Bias
Responsibility	Irresponsibility
Fairness	Unfairness
Firmness	Weakness
Industriousness	Idleness
Freedom of choice	Monopoly/Uniformity
Equality	Inequality

SOURCE: ADAPTED FROM CHIBNALL, 1977.

- One is that broadcast newsmakers pride themselves on being impartial as part of their professional ethic, and are required to be impartial by their own terms of reference: their own codes of practice and the statute/charter which empowers the BBC and commercial broadcasting. Newspaper editors will also talk about objectivity and getting the facts, in spite of the fact that articles clearly do have angles on their subject matter.
- Another reason is that the success of news operations depends on their being trusted. This trust is bound up with notions of fairness, truthfulness and impartiality so far as the audience is concerned. But again it is the manner of newsmaking which builds this trust – and it is exactly the constructed nature of news presentation that critics are unhappy about.

The Glasgow University Media Group (GUMG) has been examining television news output for over 20 years. It is clearly of the opinion that news is biased in favour of the views of certain social groups or classes, and against the interests of others.

- A *Reader* of the GUMG work (1995) refers to the ideology of news which 'requires it to be neutral, unbiased, impartial and balanced'.
- These values are said to be myths which allow broadcasters to 'trade upon the unspoken and dominant ideology of our society – the liberal notions that there is a fundamental consensus'.
- The GUMG looks at factors such as the use of language and the relative time given to different points of view. For example, it criticises the use of indirect reported speech in which a version of what someone has said is presented out of context and as if the whole thing is all of what was said originally.

In the use of reported speech, the current forms, routines and conventions of television news work unwittingly or otherwise to produce a bias against understanding of trade union and labour viewpoints.

Fiske (1987) also criticises news for bias against trade unions when he introduces Barthes's notion of *exnomination*. This draws attention to the fact that frequently the union position in a dispute is not only expressed through reported speech but also clearly identified with an individual – it is personalised; they are named or nominated. Management positions are given the authority of apparent objective neutrality: they are not necessarily shown or heard. The news person speaks for them, paraphrasing their position.

Negrine (1994) is critical of the position of the GUMG, indeed of many commentators.

- He comments that ideas about bias are relative to what one thinks *non-bias is*.
- He argues that criticisms of news coverage as being biased for lack of background coverage fail to take account of all current-affairs output, or to recognise some range in the handling of news – eg Channel 4, with its in-depth items.

Study points

1 How does news presentation work against the representation of social diversity?
2 List points about the appearance and behaviour of news presenters which work to endorse their authority and the notion of objectivity in news.
3 Identify a news story which is about conflict. Examine the story, looking at ways in which its treatment fits in with ideas offered in the section on consensus (see p 90).
   a In what ways does the consensual approach endorse the idea of stability?
   b Who is going to benefit from a consensual resolution to your conflict story, and in what way?

NEWS CASE STUDY: THE GULF WAR

For this section, the author acknowledges a particular debt to the works of **Douglas Kellner** and **Philip Taylor** in their writing on news coverage of this way, in early 1991, between a consortium of Western forces (the Allies) endorsed by the United Nations Security Council and the forces of Iraq led by Saddam Hussein.

As a news event, this war was distinctive in a number of ways. It illustrates concepts already described, and raises issues about the handling of news and its effects on the audience.

A TELEVISION WAR

People's perception of news is in any case dominated by the medium of television, as it is well attested by surveys of where the public believes it receives its news from. But, as Kellner puts it, this was 'the first war played out on TV with the whole world watching it unfold'.

A 'HIGH TECH' WAR

Military publicity managers encouraged the presentation of conflict in terms of 'surgically precise' Western technology dealing cleanly with a world political health problem. Footage from video cameras in the front of aircraft and smart bombs, with (false) accounts from the military of the effectiveness of air strikes, encouraged this view, as well as giving a sense of actuality and truthfulness to accounts of what was going on. Baldly, there were lies told about bombing efficiency: after the war, it emerged that 70 per cent of bombs missed their targets. Iraqi scud missile sites were supposed to have been wiped out – then more missiles were fired. The military was persistent in promoting a view of a clean, effective operation, and many journalists did not ask searching questions about the inconsistencies between what they were told and what they found out.

A CLEAN, BLOODLESS WAR

The Americans were particularly keen to promote this impression because of concern about the effect on public opinion of too many body bags arriving back in America. Indeed, the American media were barred from entering the base where casualties were flown in. Allied casualties were relatively light, but certainly not as few as the military news managers suggested. Accidental deaths were generally not reported.

It may be suggested that as a medium, television creates a kind of distance from its subject matter. What is seen is known to be far away and is reduced to the size of the screen. This impression would be compounded by all the detached aerial shots and the lack of real ground fighting footage. It took a stunning photo-journalist's shot of an Iraqi incinerated inside his truck on the road to Basra to bring home the horror of conflict.

VIRTUAL REALITY

It has been argued that this was a war in which reality became what television news says it was. Baudrillard notoriously commented on the war in postmodernist terms which saw form as supplanting substance. He argued that it was no longer possible to see some kind of reality and truth 'out there' as existing distinct from what the media presented. For the audience, media reporting of the Gulf War was the truth. Media reality is inextricably part of social reality.

SATELLITE NEWS GATHERING

This dominated news reporting, especially from those journalists who sought out information independently from press briefings. Significantly, American journalists were not allowed satellite dishes: the British were. So, new technology was important, but only good so far as it was allowed to be used.

THE ROLE OF CNN

This 24-hour world news service, and its reporter Peter Arnett, had a unique position in news reporting. It had a base in the Iraqi capital, Baghdad. It had a landline link to Jordan (ironically, running through military-protected tunnels), as part of an earlier deal done with the Iraqi government. The Iraqis saw the advantage in letting pictures of the war 'behind the lines' (especially pictures of destruction to civilians) out into the world. They tried their own version of news management, but it is also true to say that there was a degree of independence of news reporting. At any rate, certainly, it is unusual to see a war reported other than from 'our side'.

ALLIED NEWS MANAGEMENT

The Allied forces sought to control the movements of journalists and to shape the news that was reported. Only 200 out of 1,500 journalists were allowed into what was called the 'news pool'. These people had controlled access to battlefields, and were given press briefings by the Allied high command. They were also given video footage. Evidence of disinformation or even lies increased as the war went on. But the majority of journalists reported the military line. They wanted to keep access to sources of information. And then there are the workings of ideology: those who might question the dominant military view of the war would be identified as unpatriotic. However, there were sharp examples of how this might place journalists in conflict with their requirement to tell the truth and to be impartial. One incident involved the mistaken bombing of a baby-food factory.

'Our side' insisted that it was really a chemical weapons factory. There was every evidence – from the cameras at the site, and from the Western builders of the factory – that it was not. CNN was sharply criticised by the American government for telling the truth. A more emotive incident was when a missile blew up a bunker in which Iraqi civilians were sheltering. The official view insisted to the bitter end that the bunker was really a military command post. The journalist Jeremy Bowen and the BBC spoke clearly for all the evidence that it was not a military target, that it had been a terrible mistake (which of course the Iraqis exploited on television). It was interesting that ITN fudged the issue in its reporting, saying that Iraqi censorship made it impossible to determine the truth. We are talking here about news management by powerful interests, about the working of ideology in action, and about issues of bias and impartiality in news reporting.

PICTURE POWER

Classically, this was a news drama that dominated screens because there were so many pictures – though little of the actual fighting itself. **John Berger**, in *The Observer* newspaper (20 January 1991), remarked that 'the medium's pathological need for moving pictures delivered it into the hands of those who control access.' The journalists would do anything to get their hands on video footage, however selective this might be, and however the facts around that footage might have been concealed.

WARSPEAK

This was a news war in which notably one heard and read a corruption of language which served to conceal cruelty and suffering, and launched understanding of the event into a kind of reality hyperspace. The bombing of targets was described as the 'suppressing of assets' by the military. Few commentators tried to deconstruct this language and its intentions, let alone its effects. The very title of the operation – Desert Storm – seeks to reposition it as a natural (and therefore acceptable) event. Questions about the motives behind and need for the war were in effect made invisible. The war was personalised in terms of justice dealing with the 'butcher of Baghdad'. Economic determinations – fighting to keep Western oil supplies available and regulated – were suppressed.

BINARY OPPOSITIONS

It is no surprise to find this war being presented in terms of oppositions. News presentation constructs its narrative and its drama in terms of conflict and opposing points of view. Kellner describes news coverage as setting up a 'dichotomy between irrational Iraqis and a rational West'. One can see something of the discourse of Orientalism here – a way of looking at and giving meaning to those who live 'in the East'. There was a clear view of the just versus the unjust, the moral versus the immoral. The nominated and demonised Saddam Hussein was clearly set up as the villain of the piece, opposed to the exnominated allied leaders. General Norman Schwarzkopf might have been celebrated as Stormin' Norman via his gung ho briefing appearances, but reporting made it clear that he was just the commander doing a good policing job for 'us'.

SOCIAL CONTEXT

It also needs to be recognised that the public's understanding of the news reporting was contextualised by its social environment. Certainly, in America there was a move to endorse and raise support for the war. Anti-Saddam T shirts were on sale. Anti-Arab racist attacks were reported. A nationally televised football game showed stadium displays shouting support for the war: 'Go, Desert Shield!' Conversely, television excluded coverage of the considerable number of anti-war demonstrations.

ISSUES AND CONTRADICTIONS

The news coverage and news management by the military also raises some fundamental issues about the functions of news and the exercise of power. The doctrine of 'the public's right to know' came up against a political concept of 'only what the public needs to know'. Freedom of speech comes up against the possible threat that freedom poses to the working of the state (and by extension, its armies). The news doctrine of impartiality is contradicted by a sense of patriotic duty to support 'our boys'. The notion of the social responsibility of the press goes out of the window when it declines to question the reasons for and conduct of the war (which has nothing to do with giving away strategic secrets).

SUMMARY

Media production in general may be seen as a process in which meanings are produced through the media text. The meaning for the producer and for the audience may be different. The process of production is also a process of selection. The media may be described as manufacturing commodities, manufacturing culture and manufacturing meanings about society.

Production is driven by imperatives which are part of a capitalist system, is shaped by practices which routinise and sell the product, and is influenced by its commercial context.

News in particular is a special form of product because it purports to give us a truthful view of the world. Critiques of the news drew attention to the conflicting interpretations offered by pluralist and determinist positions; to the special language used in news; to the commodification of news; and to the operation of ideology through news.

Newsmaking is influenced by ideas within the newsrooms about professionalism, news values and an agenda which prioritises some stories above others. News presentation refers to the form or treatment of news. It includes the presenters themselves, the framing of stories in terms of an ideal of consensual solutions to social conflict, and the shaping of some stories in terms of a moral panic. This treatment of news leads to the creation of ideas about social norms and about deviancy. All the processes of selection and the devices of news form lead to a questioning of the notion of the impartiality of news.

STUDY GUIDES

Group work

1 Examine news coverage of one story across at least two each of the quality press and television news programmes. What does that coverage tell one about the notion of impartiality in the news when comparing broadcasting with the press?

2 Research ideas about deviancy and the representation of social groups in the news. How far does your evidence confirm the idea that the treatment of groups in the news contribute to the definition of norms of social behaviour, and to the containment of social conflict?

3 Examine television news coverage from a feminist perspective which attends to the following aspects of news:

   a the use of female reporters in relation to certain types of news story;
   b the numbers and roles of women who are the subject of or who appear within news stories;
   c the numbers of and images of female newscasters.

Use your evidence to deal with the following questions:

   a Are women treated differently from men within the news stories?
   b Are females reporters given 'women's stories' or 'women's angles' to cover?
   c Do female newscasters appear to enjoy equal status with men within the programmes? In what respects? If not, why not?

1 How does the idea of professionalism in news production affect the news which we receive?
2 In what ways may news served to reproduce ideas about social inequality?
3 Is news bias inevitable, given the existence of ideology?

1 Examine the treatment of a news story which has developed as a moral panic. In particular, look at the following:
   a what aspects of the story have been dramatised;
   b how the story has been developed (ie new information or new 'angles' on it);
   c what aspects of the story would appear to be verifiable from sources (ie are likely to be true), and what aspects are opinion or conjecture or factually incorrect;
   d how certain sections of society may gain or lose from the way that the story is being handled.
2 Take the ideas of consumption and manufacturing culture (from the beginning of this chapter) and apply them to the content and treatment of a magazine of your choice. Comment on what this may tell us about social experience and social reality.
3 Use ideas about the selection, construction and presentation of news as a starting point for drafting a description of your own 'alternative news programme'. Use this alternative construct to explain how existing news works within a confined agenda and produces a selective picture of the world.

6

REPRESENTATIONS, RACE AND YOUTH CULTURE

Introduction

THIS CHAPTER IS about:

- what the word 'representation' means, and why it matters
- ideas about representation, including how it constructs a partial view of people by types and how it constructs meanings about people
- representations of race: how they may diminish and make people 'different' on the basis of their ethnic origins.

WHAT IS REPRESENTATION?

In terms of what the word 'representation' refers to, there are both simplistic and all-inclusive definitions in circulation. The simplistic version says that representation are about stereotypes. The inclusive version says that representations in the media are the visible side of ideology. But there is a bit more to it than that.

DESCRIPTIONS

The word representation certainly does refer to descriptions of people that help define the typicality of given groups – teachers. But it also refers to the depiction (ie representation) of institutions – eg schools. It is not just about surface appearance, physical characteristics: it is also about the meanings that are tied to the constructed appearance – eg meanings about teachers and schools.

Table 13: *Theorists, concepts, key phrases and propositions in this chapter*		
THEORISTS	CONCEPTS KEY PHRASES	PROPOSITIONS
John Hartley	Mode of address	• The use of form which creates a relationship with the audience
Stuart Hall	Naturalisation Point of view	• The assertion of identity as being naturally true in the way it is constructed • The physical or critical position in relation to the subject
Louis Althusser/ Stuart Hall	Difference	• Representation defined in terms of the subject's differences from other groups
Roland Barthes/ John Berger	Objectification	• Turning the subject into an object in the mind, ie no longer a real person
Michel Foucault	Discourse	• Uses of language to create particular ways of understanding the subject, and excluding other understandings
Adam Briggs and Paul Cobley	Identity	• A sense of the self as represented by contrast with others in terms of power or lack of it
Stan Cohen	Deviancy	• Problematic youth: youth shown as creating social problems
Dick Hebdige	Identity: youth as fun, youth as trouble Resistance through rituals	• Polarised media representations – ideological contradictions • Youth behaviour resisting dominant oppressive culture
John Fornas	Youth as cultural phenomenon	• Youth creating culture and expressing cultural identity through use of commodities
M Brake	Identity: lifestyle Commodification and consumption	• Youth as subordinates struggling against dominant culture • Youth defined by what it consumes
Hilleri Ganetz	Private spaces Privatisation of public spaces	• Females' use of territory: gender distinctiveness

THE LOCATION OF MEANING

So, in this sense, representation is about the making of meanings. What is represented to us through the media are meanings about the world, ways of understanding the world. But then, questions which may be asked are:

- What kind of understanding do we get from a representation?
- From whom or where does it come?
- Who loses or gains by it?
- Will different people see the same representation in different ways?

As has already been pointed out in relation to ideology, it is argued that these ways of looking at things, at people, are so naturalised (mainly through the use of conventions) that they become 'the truth'.

Representations linked to meanings

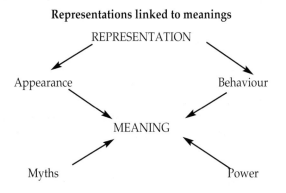

The surface of the representation of people by groups is in the appearance and behaviour depicted.
Making sense of this surface leads one to meanings about the representation. Dominant areas of meaning have to do with cultural myths and the position of that group in terms of power.

A MATTER OF POWER – IDEOLOGY

Inclusive definitions of representation are Marxist in basis. Althusser would say that ideologies are systems of representation: the one defines the other. Equally, there are views which privilege discourse as the expression of ideology, and which see representation as discourse in action. The act of representation becomes the embodiment of power relations in society. So, representations become an expression of ideology and of discourses, and what they are mainly about is power. **Adam Briggs** and **Paul Cobley** (1998) describe representation as 'a "vehicle" for transmitting ideologies in the service of maintaining/extending power relations'.

Representation and power

IDEOLOGY —▶ REPRESENTATION —▶ POWER RELATIONS

- social inequalities
- social relations
- social conflict
- social distinctiveness

> Representation is seen as an expression of ideology.
> Representation expresses different kinds of power relationship in society.
> These relationships are to do with inequalities between groups, how groups relate to one another, conflict between groups, and making groups distinctive from one another.

SOCIAL CONTEXT – HISTORY

In this case, it is argued that one can only define representation in relativist terms – in relation to the social context that produces it and which may be part of it. So, to understand what the representation of young people as flower children and hippies in the 1967 'summer of love' means, depends on understanding the social and economic circumstances behind those young people and indeed behind the news and documentary pictures of them.

PICTURES, COMMUNICATION AND REPRESENTATION

It is common to discuss representation in terms of *images* of a given subject. Indeed, a photograph may be described as a representation of X. But any language or code or means of communication may act as a means of representation. We get views of youth, age, race and so on from written articles as much as from pictures, from comics as much as from films. It is more helpful to think of representation in an active, verbal sense: it is something which is done or which happens.

Study point

What is the distinction between appearance and meaning when one talks about representation through a photograph in a magazine?

IDEAS ABOUT REPRESENTATION

THE NOTION OF DIFFERENCE

This idea draws attention to the way in which the subject is defined in terms of what it is and what it is not, in terms of how it is different from other examples. For instance, the representation of gay people as stereotypes in comedy material will concentrate on features of appearance and behaviour which are intended to make them recognisable, distinctive and therefore different from all other categories of people (or indeed people in general).

Representations can be seen as drawing attention to social difference in order to reinforce social norms – eg, homosexuality is different from heterosexuality; heterosexuality is normal.

POINT OF VIEW

Representations, especially those in visual media, are constructed from a particular point of view. The phrase 'point of view' has two meanings:

1 One refers to the literal position in space that one is placed in by the camera that has taken a photograph. This *spatial position* places one in relation to the subject and affects how one understands it. The camera position, chosen by the photographer or film maker for a reason, becomes our spectator position. For example, a high point of view at a distance from the subject has the effect of distancing us from that subject, encouraging us to be observers of the subject rather than participants. On the other hand, a shot through a doorway below the eyeline of some human subject will appear to be voyeuristic, especially if the subject is apparently unaware of 'our presence'.
2 The other understanding of 'point of view' is in terms of the *intellectual or critical position* taken in relation to the media material.

Hall (1997) describes three approaches to representation, which may be summarised as follows:

1 *reflective*: which deals with a view of or meaning about the representation which is somewhere 'out there' in our social reality;
2 *intentional*: which is concerned with the view of the creator/producer of the representation;
3 *constructionist*: which is concerned with how representations are made through language, including visual codes.

LOOKING AND OBJECTIFICATION

Here, ideas about representation are very much concerned with the visual media. It is proposed that the act of looking is also the act of making the representation apparent, giving it meaning inside one's head.

- The idea of gaze is the subject of a body of criticism. Mulvey (1975) and others have proposed that males looking at female images in films (and photographs) use a voyeuristic gaze, in which the viewer has a kind of secret power over the subject, who is in effect victimised. There has also been critical discussion about how women look at men, or how gay men look at men. Clearly, in each case, the way the looking happens, the kind of mental construct of the representation, will vary.
- Objectification through looking is another idea about the gaze. The idea here is that the subject is turned into an object. The women, the homeless child, whoever, is turned into a 'thing' in the act of representation. This act is about the gazing, as much as about the photograph or film image itself.

Study point

How does the idea of 'difference' apply to class, race and gender?

Activity

List some TV programmes in which the representation of class differences is especially relevant to the narrative or themes.

IDEOLOGY AND DISCOURSE

Representations are deeply ideological. It may be argued that the meanings about their subjects are meanings about:

- who has power and who does not
- how power is exercised
- the values which dominate the way we think about society and social relations.

So, for example, the representation of the disabled as plucky fighters against adversity may be doing some strange things to the social position of the disabled. For a start, it still draws attention to the disability, the abnormal, not the normal – to difference. It also promotes ideas about self-sufficiency and sorting out your own problems, which are ideological in themselves. The disabled may not want rivers of tea and sympathy. But some of them could certainly do with help in living a fuller life – not being left to struggle in adversity because it is the noble (or even the cost-effective) thing to do. And of course there is a discourse of disablement. Ideological positions come out of the meanings of discourses.

It may be argued that the subjects of representations (especially of stereotypes) come to personify the discourse. The idea of the hysterical female personifies not just previous Victorian ideas about madness but also present ideas about the nature of woman. It serves to support ideas about:

- women being emotional (more so than men)
- emotion being opposed to logic (men are logical)
- an excess of emotion being undesirable (whatever excess is)
- emotion being weakness (women are weak, men are not).

ECONOMIC DETERMINISM

In relation to advertising and marketing in particular, it may be said that representations are shaped according to the disposable income of the given group. Teenagers became visible when they had money to spend. Young females are presented as defining their age and gender in terms of appearance (make-up, clothes and hair products) because they spend a high proportion of their disposable income on such related products.

POSTMODERNISM

It is pretty much true to say that a postmodernist view of representation would ignore its existence, if not actually deny it. Form and referentiality are everything. The text and the reader matter. Notions of the media as having the power to do things to people are seen as simplistic, as being supplanted by the power of the text and its form, the power of reading. Certainly, people like Baudrillard more or less avoid discussions of reality by asserting that there is nothing real out there: media reality is as real as anything else. What you see is what you get.

Discussion of ideology is also marginalised, at least in terms of the exercise of power by elite social groups over others. If one takes a view that there is no absolute reality out there, then there can be no absolute measure of representations. They become relative to one another, and all have a degree of validity.

This account does not do justice to the complexities of a shift in critical thinking which is still going on. It is interesting, however, to see how postmodernism may question the notion of absolute truths, even bedrock concepts of media sociological criticism, such as ideology and representation.

Study point
Describe the contrast between a Marxist and a postmodernist view of representation.

Two theoretical views of representation

Theories about how the media work with representations	REPRESENTATIONS
DETERMINISM	construction a view of what is out there ⟶ SOCIAL
FUNCTIONALISM	reflect a view of what is REALITY out there ⟵

REPRESENTATION AND RACE

Racism through representation has a long history, reflecting on nationalism, group identity and the building of empires. Nations and smaller groups have a history of forging a sense of identity, of superiority and of difference through the ways that they represent themselves to other groups, and other groups to themselves. The fairly recent break up of the state of Czechoslovakia is an example of where identities existed and were exploited by politicians to the end of creating two nations. Ironies within this dichotomy included the disparaging by both Czechs and Slovenes of the Romany gypsy communities living in 'their' country.

McRobbie (1994) refers to representation as a 'site of power and regulation as well as a source of identity'. Representations are an expression of discourses which give meaning to the idea of race (and racism). Hegemony is about the struggle for ascendancy between these discourses, for the assumption of the power of one kind of representation over another.

Hall (1981) says that

the media construct for us a definition of what race is, what meaning the imagery of race carries, and what the 'problem of race' is understood to be. They help us classify the world in terms of race.

TWO CRITICAL POSITIONS ON RACE

It is worth reminding ourselves that there are two main kinds of critical position on the media in terms of:

• why they might construct kinds of representation of race
• how media products in general get constructed
• the relationship between media producers and the audience.

1 *Determinism (Marxism).* This would suggest that albeit unconsciously the producers construct representations whose meanings work in favour of those

who control society and often against the interests of those who are controlled and are represented. The media construct our idea of reality because they construct words and images which become at least part of that reality.

2 *Functionalism.* This would suggest that the media reflect public attitudes and give the audience what they want. If representations change over a period of time, then this in itself is a reflection of changes in public attitudes.

RACE, IDENTITY AND DISCOURSE

It may be argued that identity comes with a representation: the identity is part of the meanings generated by representing certain groups of people in certain ways. The representation in turn comes from the ideology, from its way of conceiving the world and power relations.

Discourse analysis would shift the argument subtly but significantly, and would say that:

- representations make the discourses apparent;
- ideology is bound up with discourses;
- in effect, there are only discourses;
- power operates within and between discourses: a struggle to achieve the dominance of one view or one meaning over another. Black may equal trouble if it is young males on the street; it may equal good looking and cool if it is footballer Ian Wright presenting a TV show.

It could be argued that whatever the view of the relationship between concepts of ideology, representation and discourse, the significance lies in meanings about race which are in people's heads.

Briggs and Cobley (1998) point out that our notions of race have nothing to do with objectifiable biology – they are just ideas about race. In terms of identity, they point out that it may refer to a number of elements:

- the person's own 'racial' identity (eg 'white');
- other 'racial' identities to which that person's 'racial' identity can be opposed in a power relationship (eg 'black' vs 'white');
- a discourse that asserts the centrality of race as a defining feature of a person's identity (eg racism);
- other (non-'racial') identities to which that person's 'racial' identity can be opposed/complemented in a power relationship (eg 'race' may be outweighed by 'gender').

Representation and identity

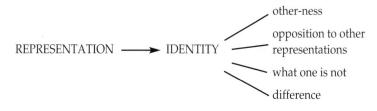

REPRESENTATION ⟶ IDENTITY

- other-ness
- opposition to other representations
- what one is not
- difference

STEREOTYPES

In one sense, it seems to be a truism that one should talk about representations and stereotypes in the same breath. But however much negative stereotypes may be the unacceptable face of representations, they are indeed the face and not the body, the substance of misrepresentation. The media may peddle notions of the black man as drug dealer or pimp, or the black woman as hooker, for example. This is stereotyping as a simplistic, reductionist description which sets up a standard of what is 'normal' – 'Everyone knows that'. Implicitly, it excludes other possibilities which fall outside its limited sphere.

It is also possible to identify categorisation by race which is recognisable but not strictly stereotypical. This is more about ways of constructing views of the quality of difference in terms of race. For example, there is:

- 'other people as victim', which comes out of images of starving children in Sudan or images of dispossessed Malawi people;
- 'other people as exotic', which is loved by fashion photographers when posing the model with a virile-looking tribesman or against the backdrop of the camel driver and his beasts;
- 'other people as threat', which co-opts a range of racial types – the fundamentalist Arab terrorist; the black youth as criminal, and so on;
- 'loose categories', but dominant ones, of the black person as social problem, as entertainer, as sportsperson.

Though there is widespread pessimism about the space for positive images of race, there are examples. Asian shopkeepers are perceived as being particularly hard-working. Comedy television programmes such as *Goodness Gracious Me* (written and performed by an Asian cast) achieve prime-time viewing, sending up both Asian and British attitudes. And music represents an interesting point of intersection between races and race images. TV programmes such as *Flava* are watched by white people as much as by black people, not least because young people have very positive images of black performers. McRobbie (1994) talks of *interactive cultural sociology* in referring to the need for more understanding of interaction between white and black youth culture, indeed for the need not to assume a separation between cultures.

NATURALISATION

Representations imply, in their construction of views, that they are endorsed by nature, by a natural order of things. Inherent in racist representations is the unspoken but emphatically understood view that whatever 'white' is, is normal. Negative connotations of 'blackness' are also held to be naturally true.

Hall (1997) ties naturalisation to the idea of difference (between 'black' and 'white') when he describes it as a 'representational strategy designed to *fix* "difference", and thus *secure it forever*'. He refers literally to Nature when describing the nineteenth-century white American view of black slaves which endorsed their slavery by placing them as children of nature, as something less than 'civilised' human beings, as born to servitude by nature. One may extend this view of the naturalising process as working to endorse inequalities of power in respect of gender, class and so on. It is as insidious to assert that women are 'naturally' better than men at looking after children, as it is to claim that black people are naturally better than white people at dancing.

RACE AND SPORT

There are strange resonances about the representation of black people in sport, not all of them negative. On the one hand, there exist stereotypical assumptions about black people being naturally good at sport. On the other hand, it may be argued that success in sport is good for the self-image of black people and promotes social integration. But then again, there are reports by black footballers of fascist remarks from the crowds (usually the opposition). Photographs of black people winning races and scoring goals are double-edged in their meanings so long as ideas of difference are still in our minds. These images stand for sporting success, and yet may confirm the illusion that this is what black people are good at. There is also the questionable colonisation of the ability of black sports people in the cause of success for the national team or for the club. The conduct of sport works in two opposing directions:

1 It works against difference when promoting the team above all else.
2 It works for difference when drawing on national and racial identification to underline the idea of competition.

In its turn, competition is a function of the marketplace – conflict makes money.

Neil Blain and **Raymond Boyle** (1998) draw attention to the fact that 'sport ... becomes deeply incorporated into people's sense of who they are and what other people are like'. In this respect, sport becomes a focal point for identity. It has a richness of representation in a very public context. They are also pessimistic about the negative meanings inscribed in representations of people in sport:

Ideologies of gender and race seem so deeply rooted, and class positions so well entrenched that … sports mediation will continue to function as a producer and reproducer of relatively conservative views of the world … .

Study point

How the success of black people in sport is understood depends on the answers to questions of meaning and of attitude.

1   Is it the case that this success is okay only because it is attached to winning for Britain or winning the FA Cup?
2   Would success still be okay if that same black person were being made Minister for Economic Affairs?
3   Are the last two questions meaningless? They would be if no sense of difference existed – but if they have meaning, this is because of the power of representation.

Study point

1   Brainstorm and list the occupations of all the ethnic minority people whom you have heard about through the media (eg footballers).
    a   Are there any patterns in your list?
    b   Is the list similar to or different from your experience and knowledge of people whom you know in your everyday life?
2   In what ways is representation about power?
3   In what ways does the use of the word 'black' in language and the use of the colour black in images contribute to negative connotations of black in the context of race?

REPRESENTATIONS OF YOUTH

Youth cultures are interesting because they not only are represented in the media but also help construct their own representation. They may be regarded positively or negatively (as in stereotypes such as comedian Harry Enfield's inarticulate, lank-haired, permanently angry Kevin). But in society, young people are great consumers and users of media and cultural artifacts, to manufacture a shifting and interlocking set of subcultural identities. As Fornas says (1995): 'Young people … express themselves to an unusual degree in text, pictures, music, styles …'.

In spite of arguments about the interchangeability of 'reality out there' and the reality of the media, it is possible to see some distinction between street culture as it is lived, media culture as it is experienced, and media culture as it is reused back in the street culture. Youth culture becomes a composite of these activities and experiences.

WHAT IS YOUTH AND YOUTH CULTURE?

Youth culture may be too much a 'taken for granted' category. It is useful to reflect on what we might mean by the phrase.

In terms of representation, Hebdige has produced the simple but recognisable oppositions of 'youth as fun'–'youth as trouble'.

Michael Brake (1985) offers us:

1 respectable youth
2 delinquent youth (usually male)
3 cultural rebels
4 politically militant youth.

though these categories (2, 3 and 4 at least) are reflexively defined because they are what researchers have been mainly interested in.

Fornas (1995) would see youth defined in three ways:

1 as a physiological phase of development;
2 as a social category formed by institutions such as school, and partly defined through rituals such as confirmation;
3 as a cultural phenomenon centering on the expression of identity.

Points of evaluation
1 If one concentrates on culture and the dominant categories of research, then gaps become apparent. Questions need to be asked, for example:
   • Where is the study of middle class white males?
   • Why has there been so much emphasis on masculine working class subcultures?
2 There is a great deal more to be investigated in relation to young females in general.
3 There is very little written on young gay people in particular.
4 Youth categories need to be reconsidered.

Bill Osgerby (1997) says: 'Rather than being perfectly framed cultural entities, subcultures have always been fluid and fragmented hybrids.'

5 The relationship between youth and the fashion, music and other media industries is a dynamic one. Notions of youth simply as victims of a consumer culture don't really stand up, though it would also be naive to assert that young people are never seduced by marketing and image.

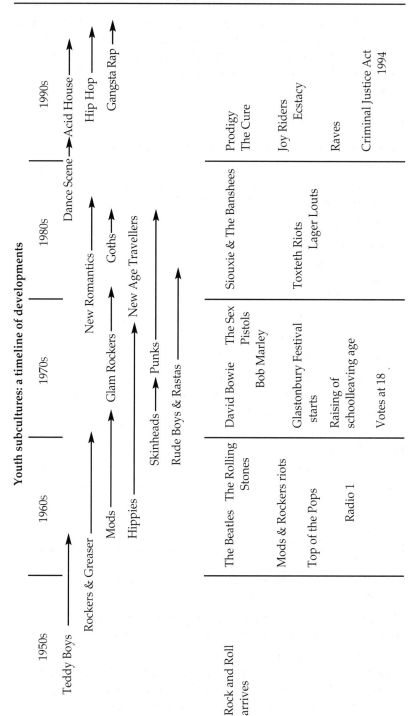

Youth subcultures: a timeline of developments

	1950s	1960s	1970s	1980s	1990s
	Teddy Boys →				
		Rockers & Greaser →	New Romantics →	Dance Scene → Acid House →	
		Mods →	Glam Rockers →	Goths →	Hip Hop →
			Hippies →	New Age Travellers →	Gangsta Rap →
			Skinheads → Punks →		
			Rude Boys & Rastas →		

Rock and Roll arrives	The Beatles The Rolling Stones	David Bowie The Sex Pistols	Siouxie & The Banshees	Prodigy The Cure
	Mods & Rockers riots	Bob Marley	Toxteth Riots	Joy Riders Ecstacy
	Top of the Pops	Glastonbury Festival starts	Lager Louts	Raves
	Radio 1	Raising of schoolleaving age		Criminal Justice Act 1994
		Votes at 18		

6 Loose assumptions about youth as teenager don't bear close examination, given that younger and older teenagers usually have very different degrees of autonomy, cultural interests and even social relationships. Teenager as a concept comes from American market research of the 1940s.

7 However one defines youth groups by music, even this may not lead to very firm ground. The 1990s British Jungle music genre crosses over definitions by class, race and gender.

8 The distinctiveness of subcultures within something called 'youth' is in any case only relative. Subcultures share some features of the more general class cultures in society, even though they also have distinctiveness. And in talking about 'youth', it is easy for high-media-profile youth groups to distract one from the truth that there are many 'ordinary' young people out there, not much in conflict with the generality of culture and society.

9 It is tempting to say that sociologists and culturalists are interested more in exceptions.

Brake (1985) gives us a formal definition of subcultures in these terms: 'meaning systems, modes of expression or life styles developed by groups in subordinate structural positions in response to dominant meanings systems'. So, youth subcultures become recognisable and distinctive when they are different, when they are struggling against expressions of power. These expressions may be seen as discourses – of school, economics, family, class.

MEDIA IMAGES AND SOCIAL REALITY

The images of youth in the media are not only selective, they also suggest a kind of cohesiveness that is not seen or felt 'out there'. Indeed, the media reflect back to young people a description of what they are, what they are doing, which then becomes assimilated and used. In this model, media reality becomes reality. But of course the media story is not simply swallowed whole. Osgerby (in Briggs and Cobley, 1998) refers to this relationship between two kinds of reality when he says: 'Media intervention … gives youth subcultures not only national exposure but also a degree of uniformity and definition.'

Daren Garratt (1997) puts it another way when he says: 'media coverage represents how they (Punks) should behave even if, largely, they haven't been.' In other words, negative media representations of youth as trouble invite youth to be trouble.

But yet another argument about media images suggests that the very fact of media publicity, of the adoption of a youth style by fashion industries, actually makes them less attractive. That is, *the subculture abandons what becomes commonplace*. Again, this was in some respects the case with punk, when high-street stores started selling clothes with sewn-in extra zips, and so on. The identity of Acid House, the subversiveness of going to a Prodigy gig, was undermined when the underground 'smiley' logo ended up for sale on the high street. However, this view suggests an alert consciousness about what the media is doing, and an intention to avoid being caught up in their games. This position broadly underlay the work of **Paul Willis** and Dick Hebdige, in the 1970s. If one likes, it is the idea that youth is in control, not the media.

The evidence doesn't really support this view. Nor does it prove that the media are simply shaping youth identities to the ends of capitalism. The dynamic relationship involved is more complicated than that, and varies, depending on which example of youth culture one is discussing.

Brake (1985) suggests that youth cultures offer an alternative form of social reality for their participants, one that provides more enjoyment and more self-esteem.

STYLE AND IDENTITY

The idea of youth as style, providing identity during a personal development phase when issues of identity and social relationships are to the fore, is very well established. It is in a sense unarguable, even if it is not all that may be said about youth cultures. As Brake (1985) puts it:

> *our social identity is constructed from the nexus of social relations and meanings surrounding us, and from this we learn to make sense of ourselves including our relationship to the dominant culture.*

Some would argue that an identity that is part of a recognisably separate subculture must produce a relationship which is one of struggle, if not downright opposition to that dominant culture. Hippies and punks could fit that model.

But it might also be argued that rather than opposition, some youth culture simply sideline the dominant culture, see it as an irrelevancy. E-tab-consuming weekend party ravers in the mid-1990s would likely fit this model, trying to ignore and evade mainstream coercive forces as much as possible.

Brake (1985) describes style as:

- image: clothes, hair, make-up
- demeanour: non-verbal behaviour
- argot: language in use

– 'an expression of identity through a deliberate projection of a self-image'. Style is an expression of belonging, but also of demarcation, distinctiveness from mainstream culture.

For the semiotic reader, style is text. For Hebdige, it is part of a semiotic guerilla warfare against forms of social control. But his notion of the coherence of youth groups, of the consciousness of opposition, now seems questionable, even if the textual deconstructions remain very important.

RESISTANCE AND SYMBOLIC INTERACTION

Again, it was Hebidge (1979) who talked of a 'symbolic challenge to a symbolic order' in his deconstruction of the style of youth culture. He was referring to the symbolism of, for example, the punks' use of safety pins. This might be seen as opposed to another order of symbolism in which safety pins are for babies, or for emergency clothing repair – but not for flaunting, not for piercing or rupturing. Certainly, the idea of youth using dress to resist authority is so familiar as to be unarguable. Schools in Britain have daily battles with pupils who subvert uniforms to undermines rules. The lengths of skirts have been the subject of tape measures. Shirts are currently hung out when the school would prefer them in. Ties are tied 'wrongly' and turn into rags of string, because it is annoying to authority.

Points of evaluation

1 The idea of 'resistance through rituals' is not peculiar to youth subcultures but familiar behaviour in youth in general. Schools recognise the 'disruptive coughing fit in the classroom' ritual or the 'hanging around in the toilets for a smoke' ritual. It isn't so much of a jump to ritual greetings with handslapping, the ritual pogo dancing of punks, and the ritual (present) repetition of the word 'wicked' as sign of cool-ness.
2 Rituals using language and behaviour clearly are a sign of identity, of distinctiveness. At what point they become a sign of defiance, of resistance to authority, is harder to pin down, and a matter for discussion. The issue here is not so much one of recognising the rituals as of asking in what ways they are resistant.

PROBLEMATISATION

In a sense, the notion of youth as problem runs through many of the subsections on the representation of youth. Youth has been defined in terms of being a distinctive social problem for well over 100 years. In the late twentieth century, there are simply more news and documentary media to bring us, more quickly and more visually, more stories about the problem of youth. Commonly, these problems are focused on specific behaviours and groups as categories – teenage pregnancies, football yobs.

The problematisation of youth largely stands for problems in society as a whole, for ideological contradictions. This is not to condone particular anti-social and criminal behaviours – perhaps violence committed against an individual by a young person. But even in such a case, one would want to ask questions about who defines 'anti-social'.

Points of evaluation

1 The idea of youth as being out of control or as needing control, is a common one when negative representations of youth are constructed.

2 This model fits an assumed generational pattern – of rebellion against parents and their beliefs.

3 It may also be true to say, at this end of a century, that the controlling forces of authority seen in social codes, class distinctions and enshrined in law, have diminished over a period of time.

4 Youth may not so simply be controlled (ie changed) by force of social beliefs or by physical coercion (ie degrees of legal protection).

5 Changes in education and the nature of work are related to a situation in which the nature of control may be questioned by young people, and work itself does not always supply an arena in which control can be exerted.

COMMODITY CULTURE

The place of youth cultures within a more general and material culture is complex. Youth is invited to consume, youth is a market, youth is turned into a commodity in itself. 'The need to consume is invented, satisfied by consumption' (Brake, 1985). On the other hand, youth is not a victim of a commodity culture when it actually invents styles, and in some cases rejects consumerism and materialism.

Garratt (1997) says of youth, 'we come into contact with their commercialisation not their formation.' So, if shops are now full of variations of the ubiquitous 'puffa jacket', then this does not describe the original phase of youth culture when this garment was first adopted.

There is a tension, but not necessarily a contradiction, between the idea of youth as independent from but also as a consumer of commodity culture. Youth cultures, in their various phases, are both of these things.

SOCIAL CONTRADICTIONS – AND SOLUTIONS

It may be argued that youth cultures are an expression of and an attempt to deal with social contradictions which affect youth. Among examples of these contradictions are the following:

• Youth is expected to take its part in a society which values individualism but practises conformity in institutions such as schools.

• Youth is expected to prepare itself for work, and is told that educational qualifications are part of that preparation. But youth also knows that the jobs market is limited and that qualifications don't guarantee jobs.

• Youth is 'told' that consumption of commodities is desirable (and a valid part of becoming an adult), but isn't offered the resources with which to consume.

- Youth experiences and sees representations of a mainstream culture in which the consumption of alcohol is commonplace, but is also 'told' that drugs are forbidden.
- Youth is asked to suppress its sexuality (in a biological period of sexual energy), but is surrounded by media representations of sexual attraction and activity.
- Youth is offered media representations of attractive and active lifestyles, but may experience fractured family life, broken local economies, which make that lifestyle unattainable.

Points of evaluation

1 If these contradictions are not dealt with by mainstream culture, then it is attractive to subvert, reject, oppose, and in various ways deal with them by creating an alternative culture that makes more sense.
2 In this way, it may be said that youth cultures are the solution to a problem.

DISCOURSE AND HEGEMONY

These terms may be used to interpret the experiences of youth cultures.

Youth may be seen as the victim of a struggle for power between discourses. Youth is caught, for example, between the discourses of childhood, adulthood and education. Adults talk inconsistently to young people as if they are children over whom they have/should have power, but also talk to them as if they should be 'grown up' and should have responsibilities. Education also wants them to remain under control and postpones the assumption of adulthood, of independence and earning power.

Representations of youth incorporate contradictions by importing language and meanings from various discourses, such as those of age or of criminality. An 18-year-old female, for example, may be a 'girl', a 'woman', a 'mother', a 'shoplifter'.

Discourses of youth are in this sense often composites of other discourses, but all in the cause of maintaining social control, of maintaining ideological positions which 'keep youth in its place'.

The dominant discourses remain those of law, masculinity and class.

GENDER

The representation of young women in the context of youth cultures has been 'overshadowed' by the apparent visibility of young men on the streets – lager louts, et al. – and by a perception that youth culture is about problematic young men. In spite of work by people like McRobbie, young women haven't had the attention from researchers.

Yet one can argue that, especially since the 1970s, young women are not really less visible. For example, the high punk era of the late 1970s displayed many young women in the streets. Their style, their involvement, was no less than the males. In the same decade, Glam Rock produced sometimes androgynous male artists and many male performers experimenting with make-up and other signifiers of feminity. Hebidge (1979) argues that the Bowie-ites here were challenging assumptions, false perceptions, and attitudes towards gender, not least in relation to working class conservatism. They were, he says, 'challenging at a symbolic level the "inevitability", the "naturalness" of class and gender stereotypes'. Bowie fans were female as much as male, but anyway, for the male it was, one may say, a way of dealing with a gender cultural change in which the girls were not really invisible or indoors or insignificant any more. How far they were (and are) equal is another argument. The commodity culture is very powerful. The 1970s also saw the arrival of the magazine *Cosmopolitan*, latching onto, trying to colonise, the lifestyle and aspirations of the new independent and professional female.

Perceptions of girls as youth are framed by discourses in which, for example, the very idea of gangs is a male one, so that girls can be there but 'not seen'. This is comparable to a kind of unwillingness to recognise that girls in groups do commit crimes of violence, and can behave in a noisy and aggressive manner. But this is not to fly in the face of various kinds of factual evidence such as arrest patterns by gender, or the fact that there *is* a female chapter, but only one, of

Signification and representation

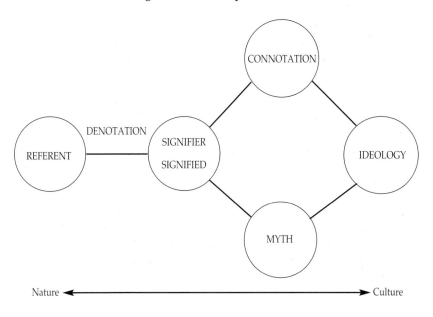

> Using a process of semiotic analysis, a representation of a young Asian woman may in denotative terms simply refer back to those three elements – young, Asian, female – without any 'baggage' of cultural meanings.
> But when the connotations which are signified are taken into account, then these may be seen to be an expression of the dominant ideology.
> In parallel with this, what is also signified are myths about being a young Asian woman. These myths too are an expression of the dominant ideology. Nature is about what is objectively true, a fact; culture is about what is constructed, a view of that young woman.

Hells Angels. Indeed, females as part of youth culture, of youth groups, are significant and active in their own way. This development is underpinned by the success of young women in education, the employment opportunities for women, and the development of an equal opportunities and feminist culture. In the 1950s, the opportunities for and visibility of young women in the public arena was limited by economic circumstances and conservative and patriarchal attitudes. The 1960s was a watershed of changing circumstances and opportunities.

It is also significant that young women have also always had *private territories* for their gathering. This is what can be termed *bedroom culture*. Girls tend to gather in this privacy to listen to music and to talk and watch videos. 'The girl's room is a free space within the family … it is a place for identity work' (Ganetz, 1995). Younger teenagers also have developed the *sleepover*, another phenomenon for building gender identity, but out of the public gaze.

These young people emerged publicly in the teenybopper phenomenon of the 1960s – Brit group fans and concert-goers. The reaction of the press showed amused fascination yet also a kind of concern that these were young women who were out there and out of control. There is a projection of desires onto the male idol, a sublimated sexuality which the media finds contradicts notions of innocence in, say, a 13-year-old. The girl as fan remains with us, though it is fair to say that gender distinctions disappear as one moves up the age range: males and females are concert-goers together as well as in their own groups.

Then there is the girls' night out, which is about gender grouping, social interaction and some degrees of public rowdiness. With girls, there is not the degree of 'pecking order' distinction that there is with boys' groups.

Hillevi Ganetz (1995) also points to the fashion store fitting room as a peculiarly female privatisation of a public space in which females share confidences free from the power and control of adults.

Stan Cohen (1997) makes the important point that females have always had a kind of cultural continuity, from being girls to being women. This continuity is seen in dominant interests of magazines for women: fashion, health, identity, relationships. The readership for magazines such as *More* and *Just Seventeen* reaches down the age group to 13- and 14-year-olds. The girls' night out might involve a group of 27-year-olds or a group of 17-year-olds.

With reference to the magazine *Just Seventeen*, McRobbie (1994) comments on the significance of the absence of romance. It replaced *Jackie* as the best-selling girls magazine. *Jackie* led on romance, on picture stories, on tales of girls competing for boys. It was a creation of the 1960s. *Just Seventeen* was a magazine of the 1980s. The representations are racially mixed, they are of girls with some power, girls who know about sex, girls who want to be in control of themselves. These are the same girls of the early 1990s who dived into Rave culture, who made Rave culture, displaying themselves but actively and on their terms. The image of Rave and other subcultures is not one that automatically conjures up males rather than females. Nor, significantly, do they invoke ideas of street violence. Girls in these groups are not defined in relation to males.

Points of evaluation

1 One should not suggest that present gender and youth culture symbolises some absolute revolution in gender politics. The 'slags or virgins' syndrome dies hard and is still imposed on girls by other girls as much as by boys.

2 Objectification through representation still dominates advertising and fashion pages, not least in the use of young female models.

3 There has been public debate about the use of young girls as 'Lolita' models, about the glorification of an asexual appearance which can only be achieved for most girls by behaviours leading to anorexia. But it is clear that the place of young women in youth cultures is significant and merits effective investigation.

4 It is also clear that social changes have taken place for young women which have changed their public image and have changed gender relationships.

5 Magazines for girls represent this change. Other examples of media representations show the conservatism of a dominant ideology.

Study points

1 In what ways is youth 'made' a problem by the media?

2 Explain the opposing views of youth as a victim of commodification, and youth as a user of commodities in the cause of identity.

3 List what you believe are key features of youth lifestyle as represented through the media. Compare this list with the experience of yourself and/or friends. What do you learn from the similarities and differences revealed by this comparison?

SUMMARY

Representation refers to the categorising of people and of ideas about them. In terms of media, it is understood dominantly through pictures, but may happen through any means of communication. The ideas represented are tied up with ideology and are particularly about the subject's place in society vis à vis power. Representations are constructed through the way the medium is used, and through that ways that we look at the subject.

Representations of race may support racism and construct an identity which is dominated by the idea of being different, the other. Such representations change with social attitudes over a period of time, but do not disappear.

The media often represent youth as delinquent or deviant. But these representations ignore the fact that many young people are not visible as subcultures on the streets or in the clubs. Even where they are visible, they are now as likely to be middle class as working class.

There is a debate as to whether the media shape youth cultures through marketing commodities, or whether youth culture generates its own style, even using commodities, which is then imitated by the mainstream music and fashion industries.

It is also argued that the appearance and behaviours of youth subcultures are a sign of resistance to the dominant culture, a sign of a struggle for power between discourses.

STUDY GUIDES

Group work

1 Take the idea of youth as colonising public spaces for private expressions of identity and values. Examples might be skateboarders around underpasses or youth in shopping precincts. Examine how this space is used and why.

2 Choose an example of ethnic minority programming from television to examine the issue of how far it seems to represent (and support) cultural distinctiveness, and in what ways it represents general cultural features. These general features may be connected with the genre of the programme – eg is a black stand-up comedian telling jokes about the shopping experience culturally distinctive in any way or not?

3 Examine the notion of contradictions in the representations of youth. Collect examples of these contradictions as expressed in the media and reinforced by social attitudes. Comment on what is revealed about social attitudes towards young people, as well as on what is revealed about the workings of ideology.

Practice questions

1 It is argued that subcultures define themselves in opposition to the dominant culture. In what respects is this true of youth culture?
2 How may the representation of ethnic groups on television contribute to a bias against those groups?
3 How do representations of British people of Asian origin construct their sense of identity?
4 How would a postmodernist view of youth culture contrast with a classical Marxist view?

Coursework suggestions

1 Investigate the representation of one social group such as the disabled or the housewife or the elderly. Focus your investigation on what meanings these representations offer about status and the exertion of power over such groups. Coordinate your study with information about such factors as spending power, socio-economic descriptors, demographics.
2 Investigate ideas about social control in relation to the emergence and performance of one example of a youth culture and its style.
3 Investigate one example of a media business in respect of the following:
    a numbers of ethnic minority employees
    b the status/jobs of these employees
    c the company's equal opportunities policies
    d government policies on equal opportunities in employment.

7

AUDIENCES, EFFECTS AND THE VIOLENCE DEBATE

Introduction

THIS CHAPTER IS about:

- how the term 'audience' may be described
- the various kinds of effects suggested by research
- the idea that audiences are addressed in different ways by the media
- different ways in which it is suggested that audiences make sense of media material (ie read texts)
- a description of the dominant approaches to audience research
- a case study of research into violence in the media and its suggested effects.

WHAT DO WE MEAN BY AUDIENCE?

The very term 'audience', which is used so confidently, poses considerable problems of definition, and carries a baggage of meanings. It suggests the idea of those who are listening or watching. It suggests a client relationship with whoever 'talks' to the audience. It suggests a set of people who become a group for the purposes of the performance received, but who indeed may have nothing else in common. There is nothing very coherent about audiences which are, as **Janice Radway** (1984) puts it, 'nomadic' – different people engage with different texts at different times for different reasons. Ironically, it is the advertising industry as much as critics of the media who may prefer to talk about the

Table 14: *Theorists, key phrases and propositions in this chapter*		
THEORISTS	KEY PHRASES	PROPOSITIONS
Theodor Adorno	Hypodermic effects	● The notion of mass audience and of passive reception
Charles Wright	Functional/dysfunctional effects	● Media institutions having a major positive or negative effect on society
Emmanuel Katz and Paul Lazarfeld	Sociability: two-step flow effects	● The importance of groups in the process of influence
George Gerbner	Cultivation theory	● The influence of the media on attitudes rather than on behaviour
Jay Blumler and Emmanuel Katz	Uses and gratifications theory	● The importance of audience needs: the idea of the audience using the media
Stuart Hall/David Morley	Dominant, negotiated, oppositional readings	● The importance of text, of decoding, of social differences, of power – in terms of how audiences make sense of the media
Pierre Bourdieu	Pleasure: cultural competence	● A link between class and taste with reference to ideology: audience pleasure driving the relationship with the media
John Fiske	Dynamic interaction	● The importance of ideology: the cultural production of meaning between media power and audience power
David Morley	Social and cultural context	● The importance of culture (including gender) shaping audience use of media, and making sense of media

audience as if the nature of audiences is agreed and consistent. Advertisers' clients want to feel convinced that they are getting value for money; that there really are well-defined target audiences out there, collections of people with definable characteristics; and that there are response behaviours to media material which clearly equal 'effects'. But the notions of 'audience' and 'effects' are much more slippery than some would allow.

As an object of study, 'audience' also has to be understood in the context of other key terms. It is commonly studied in relation to institution, text, context, technologies. In truth, one cannot understand any such key terms except by a degree of reference to the others. It is for this reason that some terms and topics are revisited in this book and looked at from different angles.

How ideology is expressed to audiences through texts

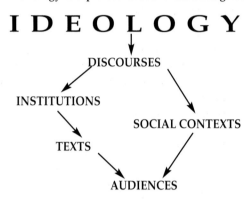

The very development of media research contains relativities and imbalances that need to be borne in mind when trying to make sense of something like effects research. In general, there is a fascination with television and its assumed power, above investigation of other media. We need, for example, to understand a great deal more about the relationship between magazines and their readers. There are, to an extent, academic fashions which shift with certain kinds of critical approach. For example, since the 1950s there has been a definite shift from assumptions about passive audiences to a belief in active audiences. But some argue that this shift has gone too far in its assumptions about audience 'independence'. There has been a shift from a keen interest in semiotic analysis and text in the 1970s, to a greater interest in audience in relation to cultural criticism in the 1980s and 1990s. But again, some commentators would pull us back to retaining an interest in how meanings are constructed into texts (preferred readings), at the same time as looking at how audiences read 'their own' meanings into texts.

It is also argued that audiences do not actually exist in a meaningful way until reading or views takes place. **Virginia Nightingale** (1996) argues that 'audiences only exist at the point of interaction with the text – not as a group in existence waiting to respond.'

MASS, GROUPS, INDIVIDUALS

Mass audience is a concept still assumed to be the natural corollary of the notion of mass media – 12 to 15 million people an episode for the soap opera, *Coronation*

Street – but this defines the audience only in terms of numbers. All we know is that many have switched on at one time to watch one programme. Of course, one does know other things, like the big proportion of women viewers for this soap.

Groups as audience is a more valid description, not least families and friendship groups, and looser sets such as fans. So, audiences (and effects) need to be understood in terms of how families watch television, and how fans talk about what they have read in 'their' magazine.

Individuals as audience is also true as a way of describing our relationship with the media. The reading of texts may well be an individual experience – watching a film in a darkened cinema, reading a newspaper on a bus, listening to a CD in one's own bedroom. Twenty thousand people may buy the same CD, but it may be that none of them know one another. Hundreds of people may be in the same concert hall, but that experience and the bands are all they have in common.

CONSUMERS AND USERS

Consumerism is associated with Marxist models of the media, and with ideas about commodity fetishism and about ideology imposing itself on the audience through media discourses. In this case, the audience is seen rather as a victim of the media. The notion of active users has more to do with critiques which favour textual and cultural analysis, which believe that audiences can make oppositional readings and can make use of media/cultural artifacts for their own ends.

WAYS IN WHICH MEDIA INDUSTRIES CONSTRUCT AUDIENCES

Audiences are defined in a number of ways by the media, not least in order to validate charging clients for advertising time and space. In the first place, descriptions of audiences will be by common notions of gender, age, occupation, region. But then there are other ways of constructing audiences:

- *Socio-economic status* is a common descriptor in which people's occupation/ status and income (especially disposable income) is described in bands A to E, with bands A to C being the wealthiest and most attractive target audience. Audiences are valued for what they can spend.
- *Television ratings* or *TVRs* – are peculiar to television and are a measure of the percentage of a given target audience that is watching the channel over a defined period of time. So there are TVRs for older children watching, in which the measure will be related to the 4.30 pm to 7.00 pm time slot.
- *Scheduling* involves categories of 'bulk audience' description in which certain kinds of audience are known to watch television in certain bands of time. For example, at 11.30 in the morning, the audience will be dominated by housewives and the unemployed.
- *Programming* implies similar descriptions and the placing of programmes at

certain times. But it also implies the definition of audiences by genres. So, chat shows appear during the day because they are cheap to produce, they appeal to a female audience, and at 4.00 pm they also pick up a return from the school audience.

- *Readership and circulation* define audiences for print media in terms of those who read and those who buy. Often, more people read than those who buy a magazine – a selling point to advertisers.
- *Lifestyles* have been a popular way of describing audiences to the industry for the last 15 years. These profiles of 'types' describe people in terms of the place they live in, the goods they consume, their relationships and their leisure habits, as well as basic things like income. This characterises consumers as social types, and makes it possible to sell a suite of goods to them.
- *Psychographic profiles* define the audience in terms of their sense of identity and their values. A version of these profiles for younger audiences appears in Table 15. Clearly, psychological and social descriptions of audiences are constructed from research in order that media material can itself be constructed to appeal to these 'groups'. There is no argument here about intentionality – ie an argument that meanings are inscribed within a text on purpose. Nor is there an argument that mode of address matters.

Table 15: *Psychographic variables: younger 'types'*	
Trendies	Those who crave the admiration of their peers
Egoists	Those who seek pleasure
Puritans	Those who wish to feel virtuous
Innovators	Those who wish to make their mark
Rebels	Those who wish to remake the world in their image
Groupies	Those who just want to be accepted
Drifters	Those who are not sure what they want
Drop-outs	Those who shun commitments of any kind
Traditionalists	Those who want things to stay as they are
Utopians	Those who want the world to be a better place
Cynics	Those who have something to complain about
Cowboys	Those who want easy money

SOURCE: SELBY AND COWDERY, 1995.

GENDER

The definition of audiences in terms of gender relates to feminist analysis of the media. There is a considerable body of critical literature which attends to 'female texts' such as romance or womens' magazines, and to how women use texts. There is evidence that, for example, men prefer factual material on TV such as news, whereas women prefer affective material such as drama. Or again, it seems that men prefer to view with undivided attention, whereas women may dip in and out of viewing or be happy to break off and comment on what they are watching.

Study points

1 In what ways may it be argued that the concept of a mass audience for the media is a false one?
2 Do audiences actually exist, apart from when they are interacting with media material?
3 In what ways do notions of audience overlap with social groups or categories?

WHAT DO WE MEAN BY EFFECTS?

In some ways, it may seem obvious that effects of the media have got to be *behavioural* or *attitudinal* – ie influencing what we do and what we think. But categorising effects is as difficult as measuring them. It is nearly impossible to distinguish the media from other social, biological, psychological and environmental variables, as specifically causing something to happen. Having said this, certainly one can point to some effects which might be better described as *results*, to distinguish their specificity and immediacy. The BBC raises millions of pounds for the Children in Need charity every year. There is no argument that the direct pleas on television result in people pledging money. Similarly, there is no doubt that a programme like *Crimewatch* results in people sending information which causes criminals to be caught. What the effect of such programmes is on conceptions of poverty or of crime is a different matter.

Effects models and effects research demonstrate the problems of defining effects, of accounting for an almost infinite number of variables, and of constructing theories which are not so hedged about with qualifications as to be meaningless. More is said about these problems in the last section below about violence and the media.

HYPODERMIC MODELS

These are the classical effects ideas contained within the metaphor of the audience's being injected with ideas by the media. They largely stem from ideas of the Frankfurt School and writers such as **Herbert Marcuse** and Theodor Adorno (though it is fair to say that they reassessed if not fundamentally changed their views over a period of time). The production, flow and reception of ideas is seen as being relatively unproblematic. Contradictorily, while few people accept this model, still it persistently emerges through the media as a simplistic way of explaining tragic and violent public events in particular. The murder of James Bulger by two boys little older than he was , was 'blamed' by some of the press on the boys' having watched a film called *Child's Play*. The fact that there was no evidence that they had watched the film didn't stop the persistence of this 'hypodermic' view that somehow they had been injected with violent ideas by the media. The irony is of course that these very news reports themselves may have the effect of causing readers to believe in the idea of simple cause and effects.

In fact, such idea of effects were rejected as early as 1960 when Joseph Klapper summarised the inconclusiveness of research to date:

Mass communications ordinarily do not serve a necessary and sufficient cause of audience effects, but rather functions among and through a nexus of mediating factors and influences Quoted in Philo, 1990.

FUNCTIONAL/DYSFUNCTIONAL

The idea that the media have positive and negative functions was a popular one during the 1960s. Given that the word 'functions' has become largely conflated with the word 'effects', the idea still makes sense as a way of describing what is going on, especially since it can embrace contradictions. For example, **Charles Wright**'s *Functional Inventory* would include the idea that the media both promote a mass culture and yet also preserve subcultures. This matches a present situation in which one can see both broadcasting and narrowcasting at the same time.

SHORT TERM/LONG TERM

Effects can be categorised as being more or less immediate on the one hand, or long term (and probably diffuse) on the other. Broadly speaking, this is a distinction between believing in immediate *behavioural* effects (eg copycat violence) and longer-term *attitudinal* effects (eg as influencing beliefs and values regarding violence). But the idea of short-term effects has been discredited because generally there is no evidence for them. Copycat violent episodes, for example, are an exception not a rule, and they are always associated with other factors such as personality disturbances or adverse social circumstances.

The idea of long-term effects on social attitudes is attractive in principle but also very hard to demonstrate in practice, not least because really long-term research isn't being funded (without going into other methodological problems). All the same, it is these longer-term and ideological effects – eg attitudes towards gender – which in principle it would be correct to be concerned about. It is the 'drip drip' notion of accumulative effect which is behind some of the arguments about cultural effects, especially those to do with the acquisition of identities.

PASSIVITY / ACTIVITY

In spite of the popularity of phrases like 'couch potato', there is now a lot of evidence of active effects on audiences, including participation in sports such as American football following screen exposure of the sport, and socially active discussions around drama series (see the section on audiences reading texts on pp 143–7).

TWO-STEP FLOW AND THE INFLUENCE OF GROUPS

Emmanuel Katz and **Paul Lazarfeld** (1955) produced a two-step flow theory of media influence and effects, based on the social context of audience reception. Briefly, they suggested that the first step was the construction/mediation of material by some significant media person such as a newscaster – the *opinion maker*. The second step was the reception of media material by a 'significant' member of social groupings – the *opinion leader*, the person whose opinions were listened to by those around them. Members of the audience were therefore affected by the media third hand, and under the influence of peer groups.

INTERACTIONISM

Fiske (1987) argues, as do others, that the term 'effects' is synonymous with hypodermic theories about what the media do to audiences. Since the hypodermic theory is discredited, in academic circles at least, it follows that the idea of effects is largely meaningless as well. So far as he is concerned, there is a dynamic engagement or interaction between text and audience, which produces meanings.

Philo (1990) says

The cultures of any given moment are part of a social process in which beliefs are produced and contested in the conflict between groups and classes.

USES AND GRATIFICATIONS

These describe effects in terms of individual needs gratified by use of the media. As an idea, it fits the active audience model.

Jay Blumler and Emmanuel Katz (1974) describe four kinds of need:

- *surveillance* – ie getting information on what is going on in the world;
- *diversion* – ie a break from routine and work;
- *personal relationship* – ie talking about relationships through the TV experience;
- *personal identity* – ie exploring oneself through reflection on the programmes.

The first two items also appear in functionalist inventories of what the media do.

Other commentators have criticised the gratifications model for its assumptions of an open, pluralistic choice of material and how this could be read, and for not taking sufficient account of the social context involved in using the material.

CULTURAL/IDEOLOGICAL EFFECTS

Comment on this idea permeates much of the material of this chapter, and indeed the rest of the book. For example, moral panics might be described as having the effect of needlessly raising public anxiety about events and forms of social behaviour. If one accepts that ideology works through representations to shape public perceptions of social groups, then stereotyping is also an effect of the media. Fiske (1987) says:

Television does not 'cause' identifiable effects in individuals; it does, however, work ideologically to promote and prefer certain meanings of the world, to circulate some meanings rather than others, and to serve some social interests better than others.

Points of evaluation

1 Ideas about the effects of the media have moved from transmission models to interactive models – from messages going from the media to meanings being made between audience and text. This raises questions about how audiences interact with media and under what conditions.
2 A parallel shift in ideas is that from the passive to the active audience. The question raised is: what kind of activity?
3 The sheer number of contextualising influences (variables) on the audience causes some commentators to question whether effects can be measured at all.
4 The effects of the media do not appear to be all negative. Yet those reported are mainly negative. This raises questions about social attitudes towards effects and media behaviour in reporting them.
5 If effects are attitudinal as much as behavioural, then this raises two questions: how may one best measure attitudes; and how are those attitudes then to be related back to social behaviour?

6 Effects may be a group experience or the result of group influence on the individual. The issue then is how far effects are an individual or a collective phenomenon.

Moral panics and the reinforcement of deviancy

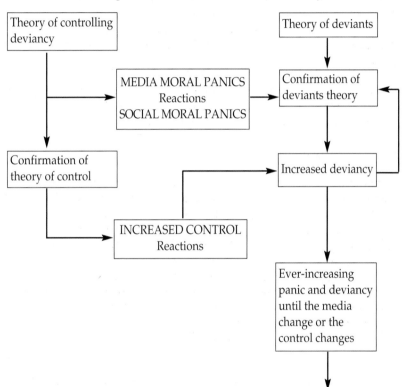

Moral panics emerge from ideas about social control – especially the media as an agent of social control. The 'evidence' of panic in the media seems to confirm the theory of deviancy, including the idea that control needs to be exerted over the deviants.

However, both the control and the media moral panic are likely to lead to increased deviancy. This may become a vicious circle or a self-fulfilling prophecy – until the moral panic subsides for lack of media coverage and/or because ideas about how to control the deviancy also change.

SOURCE: ADAPTED FROM COHEN, 1985.

ADDRESSING AUDIENCES

Just as audiences may engage with a text and make meanings from it, so also there is a sense in which the text teaches out to the audience. Texts are not neutral, least of all ideologically. So if they are inflected, then these inflections are made by someone, intentionally or otherwise. This book is a text which did not fall into place by accident. It is written with an audience in mind. It is written in a certain way.

MODES OF ADDRESS

The concept of mode of address has been explained earlier in this book. In this chapter, one might attend to different styles of address related to different audiences. The style is the effect of different uses of different codes – verbal, visual, non-verbal.

Sometimes, address is literally just that:

- *Direct address* – here, the writer addresses the reader in the first person – eg the holiday programme presenter addresses the views.
  The tone of address, the audience positioning, is in many media examples set up by an:
- *Initial address*: this refers, for example, to the film title sequence, to the TV presenter's introduction, to the magazine cover. In the case of the magazine, the way that a cover face looks at us, the way that the contents previews are written, say things about the kind of reader we are meant to be, the kinds of things that we are meant to be interested in.
- *Objective address* is quite common in a range of material, such as drama, where the audience is not so specifically identifiable, or where it is intended that we should be informed. The extreme example of this is the authoritative address of news.
- *Familiar address* is the style of narrowcasting for specific audiences, in which knowledge and situation are shared through a common interest, as with a computer magazine using colloquial language and an anecdotal style.
- *Intimate address* is a more extreme version of familiarity in which the addresser engages the addressee in an almost conspiratorial fashion, excluding the rest of the world. Young women's magazines invoke teenspeak and a mixture of fantasy and real reader pictures as a key to this mode of address. Quiz and game show hosts also use devices such as the planted camera in the living room to construct an intimacy in which the studio and the home, the studio audience and the viewers at home, are brought into an intimate relationship. Some radio presenters are valued for their ability to talk in a way that makes the listener feel that they alone are being addressed.

Of course, the whole thing is an illusion. But the point is to engage the audience, to construct a relationship between text and audience, to construct an identity for that audience.

POWER AND IDEOLOGY

There is an argument that addressing the audience through the media is in itself an exercise in power. The nature of media power has been discussed in Chapter 2. The classical Marxist argument about the invisible power of ideology is expressed through the notion of false consciousness: in effect, the audience colludes in reproducing the inequalities of the status quo not so much against its will as against its knowledge of what is really going on.

Some take the view that the text is nothing but potential meaning, until it is decoded by an audience. This would seem to shift the power of meaning into the control of the audience. But the counter-argument is that, while the audience may have the power to unlock the cupboard door of the text, it doesn't have so much control over what comes out of the cupboard, or indeed over what has been put into it in the first place.

Morley (1992) frames the argument in terms of 'the difference between having power over a text and having power over the agenda within which the text is constructed and presented'. He argues against simplistic 'textual determinacy', but nevertheless says that:

The power of viewers to reinterpret meanings is hardly equivalent to the discursive power of centralised media institutions to construct the texts which the viewer then interprets; to imagine otherwise is simply foolish.

Morley is arguing against overoptimistic interpretations of the active audience, against equating this activity with a power to match that of the media, while still allowing for a degree of resistance.

Make a list of differing genres of TV programmes, describing the style in which they address their audiences, and summarising the features which describe that style. Create three headings across the tope of your page: 'Title', 'Style of address' and 'Examples of features'.

AUDIENCES READING TEXTS

How audiences read media texts, what sense they make of these texts, what they do with what they draw from the text – these are all fiercely contested by critics. One argument, that a text is so constructed that it can only be made sense of in one way, leads to the notion of *preferred readings*. That is, one meaning is preferred above others. This links to notions of power over the audience.

Questions of intentionality and of consciousness are involved. The fact that one has what is a relatively close text, which it is only possible to make sense of in one way, does not mean that the producers consciously intended to limit meanings. But given the naturalisation that takes place as hegemony operates, it is just as arguable that the producers would say: of course, there is only one way to tell this news story.

Audience readings of/responses to media are extremely complicated, in a variety of ways. The homogenised mass audience of the Frankfurt School does not really exist. There are subtle subcultural divisions within the population which produces a huge range of responses to something like a Coca Cola advert. Even if one could agree on a definition of a cultural group – educated Edinburgh Lowland Scot middle class middle-aged soft radical environmentalist – still one could not be sure of consistency of response.

This complexity is recognised by **Roger Silverstone** (1994) in discussing the relationships between ideology, audience and text. There is a struggle to retain notions of cultural domination by media over audience, in the face of arguments for the audience seizing some cultural initiative of its own from the texts. Silverstone criticises Fiske for seeing television as a kind of 'cultural democracy' from which audiences could pick and choose – 'Fiske seems to mistake ambiguity for polysemy, textual open-ness for lack of determination.' Indeed, Silverstone also rejects the idea of active audiences – 'Activity can, and does, mean too many different things to too many different people.'

Nightingale (1996) rejects the idea of 'response':

… the activity of the audience need no longer be conceived of as response, but can be better understood as symbiotic or interactive.

ACTIVE AUDIENCES – OPPOSITIONAL READINGS

But this disagreement does not mean that the idea of the active audience is invalid. In one respect it goes back a long way into the notion of different types of reading, formulated by **Frank Parkin**, reused by Hall and developed by Morley – visualised in the diagram. It is argued that audiences from certain social contexts

Reading two current affairs programmes: occupational groups as a factor

SOURCE: MORLEY, 1980. THE READINGS OF TWO EDITIONS OF A CURRENT AFFAIRS TV PROGRAMME ARE ILLUSTRATED ABOVE AND BELOW THE LINE. CLASS APPEARS TO BE LESS OF AN ISSUE THAN CULTURAL EXPERIENCE.

may read texts oppositionally. Of course, whether one is talking about an opposition, a negotiated (alternative) or a dominant (preferred) reading, there is an argument about how one might 'expect the text to be read', or about how one measures an 'agreement about the dominant meanings of the text'. Judgements of how audiences read texts and what they do with what they have read are complicated by a number of factors. These factors have not been adequately dealt with by research. Here are three examples:

- Audience response to texts are evidently more than of the 'yes/no' variety. People respond in different ways to different part of the same novel for different reasons.

- One should not conflate the immediate experience of reading the text with the longer-term effects of the reading. To read accounts of the Holocaust may move one to pity and disgust, but this does not determine the reader's future behaviour towards Jewish people, German people or humanity in general.
- One cannot always assume that texts are open, or capable of a wide variety of interpretations. Some are less open than others. Partial and persuasive communication, such as marketing material, in effect tries to close down the reading possibilities for the audience. As Morley (1992) says, one should not 'underestimate the force of textual determinacy in the construction of meaning from media products'.

THE IMPORTANCE OF CONTEXT

The physical and social environment in which audiences engage with media can potentially make a lot of difference to effects and understanding. At home, someone can read a magazine and engage in conversation about it with someone else. On a train, the reading is a solitary experience. Watching a movie is a collective social experience, while watching a TV programme may well be a more family social experiences. Even different households provide different kinds of context. **Bob Hodge** and **David Tripp** (1986) exemplify an approach to engagement with the media which is about social experience as context, in which TV helps children make sense of the world and is part of their world. Their approach sets aside assumptions about TV having an effect on children and indeed the idea of children using TV. They only interact with it. Nightingale (1996) says of this approach (and of Radway's research into women reading romantic fiction):

... instead of measuring the effects of the media on people's behaviour, the effects were proposed to lie in people's lived relationships with popular texts.

PLEASURES

The act of being an audience and a reader, it is argued, gives different kinds of pleasure. The pleasure of viewing or of reading is not simply to be equated with entertainment – which is something that the media try to do for us. The quality of pleasure has a lot to do with who we are and what are our circumstances. There is a pleasure in reading a book, on one's own, away from the demands and interruptions of others. Equally, there may be pleasure in sharing the viewing of TV chat show and exclaiming to others about the outrageousness of the participants. The quality of that pleasure, the pleasure effect, is different in each of these cases. Pleasure may vary by the gender of the reader – males viewing a football match as opposed to females watching *Emmerdale* – but clearly the effect of social pleasures is mixed up with the textual pleasures. Friends will go out together to see a movie and enjoy it, people will discuss together what they have read in a newspaper. Indeed, the stream of video screenings as part of a teenage sleepover party is as much an adjunct to the social experience as the social interaction is a spin-off from the video.

Radway (1984) examined the pleasure that women gained from reading romantic fiction. Put rather simplistically, this was seen in terms of escapism and of reconstructing reality, not least the reality of gender relations. The pleasure, the effects, are both in the act of reading and in the meanings made from the reading. There is a sense of engaging in an act of resistance through reading. It seems that a degree of common (ie gender) experience leads to one common effect of the reading, even though Radway's subjects were not part of some interacting social group.

Bourdieu (1984) introduced the idea of *cultural competence* to argue that people's pleasure in the media is defined along class lines: that notions of taste are part of this competence. Morley in particular later took on this concept and used it to make sense of the different ways in which men and women read media texts – in effect, an idea of different 'gender cultures'. Ironically, it was Morley's research which also seems to deny Bourdieu's proposition that readings and class are interrelated.

GENDER AND RECEPTION

The idea of gendered engagement with media material has just been referred to. Clearly, this is a significant interest of feminist media study, which argues that females read texts in different ways from males and under different circumstances. Many women talk during programmes, while some men prefer silent viewing. Women will view in a fragmented fashion (not least because of domestic demands on their time) while men prefer undivided attention. Men have been found to use TV remote controls as an instrument of power, to determine what is viewed – news, for example – while women are denied this power (see Morley, 1992).

Study points
1   What is the difference between preferred readings and oppositional readings?
2   What factors constrain audience choice in making sense of media texts?
3   What are some of the differences between viewing a film at home and viewing in a cinema?

Points of evaluation

1 If audiences interact with the media rather than receiving messages from them, then this may change ideas about the nature and degree of media influence.

2 The reading of media material will be affected by context. But then the problem is to define context and its influence (eg cultural, environmental, social, societal?).

3 There seem to be gender differences in the ways that texts are read. There is a question of how far these differences are significant in terms of ideology and the exercise of male power.

ASPECTS OF AUDIENCE RESEARCH

Roland Lorimer (1994) describes seven approaches to the study of audiences, summarised as follows:

1 **Effects research**: this is essentially about the notion of audience reception, though it is refined to try to take account of factors such as the context of reception. It includes the notion of cultivation analysis (see Gerbner, 1969) – analysis of texts to identify factors which may cultivate a particularly positive attitude towards a certain viewpoint. Effects research has been much preoccupied with the effects of political communication or the effects of violence.

2 **Uses and gratifications research** (see above): this turns to the needs of the audience as driving interaction with the media. In fact, research tends to assume the needs and then actually looks back to what may be in the media text that answers those needs. So it ends up dealing with the media as much as with the audience.

3 **Cultural studies** (see Chapter 3): this draws on developments in Marxist critiques of the media, and is much concerned with the ideas of representation and identities tied up with the uses of 'cultural goods' by audiences/sections of society. Textual reading and the power of ideology (ie dominant values) are important in an approach which actually synthesises ideas about influence on audiences and audiences using media.

4 **Feminist research**: this area is concerned with cultural studies, but with a commitment also to investigation of gender readings and the influence of gender factors on the interaction between media and audience.

5 **Reception analysis**: this area is concerned with the specific social circumstances in which reading takes place. This should be related to what is called ethnographic research. It would relate back to comments above on gender differences in the reception of media.

6 **Structuration theory**: in this case, Lorimer cites the work of **Anthony Giddens** (1994) and its attempt to reconcile the two dominant and apparently opposing

views which privilege either the power of the media or the power of the audience. The essence of the argument is that cultural production is to be understood in the context of talk – how talk organises understanding and meaning, and creates a structure that organises the relationship between discourse and cultural objects. These structures are actively produced within society, as opposed to the idea of given structures within which audiences have to operate.

7 **Institutional research**: this is taken to refer to what the media themselves do to investigate audiences. The concepts of *reach, share* and *time spent* are important to media, which live by their ratings figures and the amount they can charge their advertisers. There are also varieties of descriptions of audiences, as in the references to lifestyles and psychographic profiles above.

Ethnographic research is that approach in which the engagement of subcultures with media material is investigated, usually by sharing that experience of engagement, and certainly by asking the audience sample to talk about their experiences within a more or less firm agenda of questions. The study of female or child audiences by these means would be valid examples of this kind of research.

Silverstone (1994) refers to three dimensions of this approach from his own studies of families and TV viewing:

1 the description of what is going on when viewing happens;
2 the dynamics within the family of use of media (eg by age or gender);
3 the consequences for individuals and for the family as a whole.

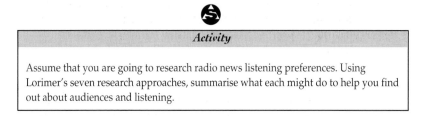

Activity

Assume that you are going to research radio news listening preferences. Using Lorimer's seven research approaches, summarise what each might do to help you find out about audiences and listening.

VIOLENCE AND THE MEDIA

In terms of research into media effects, violence, especially that related to child viewing, has always been a high-profile subject. Assumptions about the ill effects of the media, not least by the media themselves, are pervasive. Yet it will be seen from what has already been said in this chapter, that the idea of the media straightforwardly having effects on the audience, especially immediate effects, is a non-starter. However, this won't stop many people believing that it is clearly bad for people to watch 'violent' films, watch 'too much' television, listen to 'mindless' pop music, read 'rubbishy' comics, and so on.

But some of the implications both of beliefs about the media and violence, and, to some extent, of the research itself are interesting:

- People prefer to see simple causal relationships (between media and social behaviour) rather than accept complex connections between a variety of social and cultural factors.
- People look for blame and responsibility as much as for neutral causes (see the ideas behind attribution theory).
- 'Blaming' the media for violence is a form of displacement activity which diverts attention from other social causes and conditions which may predispose some groups towards violent behaviour.
- Outbursts in the media about violence are a form of moral panic which helps sell newspapers or promotes audience ratings.
- Recurrent anxieties about violence by the young or the possible promotion of violence to the young fit in with ideas about ideology and social control. They provide an 'excuse' for reasserting power in some way – revised forms of sentencing for youth, or making parents legally answerable for the behaviour of their children.

RESEARCH – THE MEDIA AND VIOLENCE

Cecilia Von Feilitzen (1998) describes four research perspectives, and summarises evidence, on the media and violence.

1 *A traditional model of the effects of media violence.* This is described in terms of a growth in longitudinal studies and in attempts to allow for other factors as having effects. In general, assertions about evidence are as follows:
    - The media have a small part to play in bringing out violent and aggressive behaviour.
    - Personality, socio-cultural background, and home, school and peer groups all have far more impact on behaviour.
    - There is some evidence that it is violent people who seek out violent media material.
    - There are distinctions between different kinds of aggression – eg physical or verbal – which seem to matter.
    - There are issues of the outcomes of violence which matter – eg the smashing of plates in a drama may release tension.
    - There is some evidence for the media creating expectations of lifestyle which are frustrated, and that this leads to aggression.
    - There is some evidence that media material of various 'exciting' kinds may create a general arousal which can then be transferred into a dominant mood, not necessarily one of aggression.

2 *The power of culture.* In this area, evidence is presented to suggest that the media can:
- arouse general anxiety about levels of violence in society
- identify some violent events as being more important than others
- legitimise perceptions of those who 'should' be the perpetrators or the victims of violence.

3 *The active audience.* There is some evidence for the following, albeit hedged about with qualifications as to methodology and disentangling a complex of influences:
- Some TV viewers seem to choose programmes to regulate their emotional state.
- The viewing of violent material may be a way for young males to measure their relative toughness within the peer group.
- Women who have been victims of violence view depictions of violence as more disturbing than do other women, and do not focus on other elements of drama.
- Factors such as membership of an ethnic group will affect readings of violence.

4 *Economies and power relations in society.* In this case, the interest is in industry and institution, power relations and economics. The economic influence of the American media industries in particular allows them to express their cultural perspectives which inform the nature of violence in both news and entertainment. The following is suggested:
- Violence in American products stems from dominant cultural values and from economic factors driving the media industries (violence makes money).
- The objects and subjects of violence are culturally based. For example, in Japan heroes suffer, but in America it is always the villain who suffers more violence. In addition, American programmes contain more violent episodes than European ones.
- Media perspectives on violence are always in line with 'official' state perspectives on the subject, particularly on 'legitimate' violence.

The Newson Report (1995) – *Children & Violence* – commissioned by the Gulbenkian Foundation involves an investigation of children and violence in society in general. It was stimulated by the murder of the child James Bulger by other children. It was not just concerned with the effects of the media, but this part of the report dominated media coverage. The Report is a very useful example of:

- the misrepresentation of research evidence by the media;
- the skewing of the evidence itself on the basis of false assumptions about other research;
- the cultural persistence of the belief in an effects model;
- assumptions about the nature of the vulnerability of children, in particular, to the depiction of violence in media material;

- how the production and reception of research is carried out in a given cultural climate.

What the Report actually asserted was that:

- violence and sadism was now more easily available via films in cinema and on video;
- this material led to real-life violence such as the murder of James Bulger;
- films had changed in respect of causing the viewer to identify with the perpetrator of violence;
- there is a great deal of research done which clearly links media violence, though heavy viewing, to violent and aggressive behaviour;
- the situation is bad and will get worse;
- the arguments for media effects are supported by the vast amount of money spent on advertising.

These assertions have no evidence to support them, nor did the Report produce that evidence. The concerns behind the Report were no doubt genuine enough, but in essence they were founded on beliefs, not on facts.

Martin Barker and **Julian Petley** (1997) provide a detailed critique of the Newson Report and of the ways that the violence debate is handled by the media. One point they make is that the phrase 'media violence' is meaningless because the various depictions of violence which underpin the dominant content-analysis approach (ie involving an incident count) are so different according to the type of programme or of medium that they cannot be talked about together. As Barker puts it:

> *I challenge the research tradition to show a single reason why we should treat cartoons, news, horror, documentaries, police series, westerns, violent pornography and action adventure as having anything in common.*

Another point made is about viewer 'identification' with characters. Barker argues that the notion of identification is a claim and a proposition that needs to be tested, because no one can see identification happening. If it does happen, then it is in the head. When he investigated research into such identification, he found that there was little of it, and that the only two examples he found which sought to check on the process of identification came up with no evidence that this process was happening.

The sheer volume of work on media effects and violence makes it difficult for some to accept that much of the work is either invalid or only partially valid. But unless the objections involved can be logically refuted, this must be the case. These objections are themselves now considerable in number, as the next section attests.

1   In what respects could it be in the interests of various social groups to regard the media as being dominantly responsible for violent behaviour?

2   Taking the example of a young male reading comics with violent images and episodes in them, make a list of all the variables or conditioning factors which are likely to influence his reading of these comics.

3   Make a grid to compare depictions of violence in fictional and factual television. Contrast them in terms of the content and the treatment. Does your completed grid suggest that it is more likely that one or the other kind of television will influence audiences into violent attitudes/behaviours?

PROBLEMS WITH RESEARCH INTO VIOLENCE

David Gauntlett (1998) provides a hard-hitting critique of 'Ten things wrong with the effects model', with particular relation to violence and children.

1   *The effects model tackles social problems backwards.* It does not start with the social violence which is the point of reference and then work towards media usage.

2   *The effects model treats children as inadequate.* Largely as a result of assumptions made from within theories of psychological development, it is assumed that children do not or cannot 'cope' with media violence. Research that deals with children's responses suggests otherwise.

3   *Assumptions within the effects model are characterised by barely concealed conservative ideology.* Most noise about media violence is made by commentators who demonstrably start from a conservative position on the potential of media for encouraging violence.

4   *The effects model inadequately defines its own objects of study.* Definitions of what is anti-social or violent behaviour in media are sometimes partial and highly questionable.

5   *The effects model is often based on artificial studies.* The methodology of study - eg the artificiality of laboratory experiments – may undermine the conclusions.

6   *The effects model is often based on studies with misapplied methodologies.* Inconsistencies and false correlations are cited by Gauntlett as examples.

7   *The effects model is selective in its criticisms of media depictions of violence.* Research is dominated by attention to fiction, rather than looking at news and violence, for example.

8   *The effects model assumes superiority to the masses.* Just as people interviewed about media effects tend to deny these, so also researchers themselves take a superior, detached attitude to effects on themselves and how these may influence their work.

9 *The effects model makes no attempt to understand meanings of the media.* Assumptions about a clear message from the media, as well as about the detached ability of the researchers to identify that message, ignore the complexity of meanings produced and then adduced by media users.

10 *The effects model is not grounded in theory.* Assumptions about effects are simplistic and too often founded on assertions. Contexts, reasons for media behaviour, and other questions about what is going on are largely ignored.

Study points

1   What does a critique of the effects model say about: the audience, the nature of violence, and methods of investigation?
2   Whether one takes an effects view of media violence and influence, or other approaches, it seems that there are questions about power and ideology behind such approaches. Whose power? Exercised how? Over whom?

SUMMARY

The definition of audience is not as simple as it may seem. There are many different ways of profiling audiences, by number or by psychological characteristics, for example. Some argue that audiences don't exist until they are interacting with the media.

The definition of effects is equally problematic because psychological effects cannot be 'seen', and behavioural effects may appear from a great range of other influences acting on people at the same time as the media. It is no longer believed that the media simply do things to people. If they have an effect at all, it is in combination both with other cultural factors and with the activities of the audiences themselves.

Audiences are addressed by texts in various styles and with the effect of positioning the audience to some degree in terms of how it will make sense of the text.

Audiences read texts in a great range of ways, some fitting in with the supposed intentions of the media, some not. It seems that audiences may interact with media to satisfy needs and to gain pleasure, but always in ways which are complicated by factors such as context and gender. This is disagreement about the ideological power in the text, as opposed to the power of the audience-reader. There are a variety of audience research approaches which relate to macro theories of media influence in general, and to micro interests in the behaviour of particular audiences.

The evidence of research into violence in the media, and critiques of this research, reveals that simple effects models are inadequate. Even elaborate models of effects become questionable due to the sheer number of variables affecting any 'reading' of violent material.

Research into violence falls into dominant areas such as effects, cultural attitudes, audience profiles/responses, institutions and ideological factors.

A key problem in evaluating violence and its effects is the research methodology used, sometimes combined with flawed assertions of proof – beliefs, not evidence, leading the outcomes. Nevertheless, social anxieties about violence remain to be dealt with, and improved methodologies may yield results in terms making some connections between media violence and social behaviours, not necessarily of a causal nature.

Group work

1 Take a magazine such as *GQ* or *More*. Examine the ways that it addresses its audience through dealing with the following questions and tasks:

  a Who explicitly or implicitly talks to the reader (eg editor, named journalist, exnominated production team, celebrity)?

  b What are illustrations used for? (For example, to explain things in an article, to add excitement, to include readers, to show how many famous people the magazine is supposed to know?)

  c Read out loud a selection of articles, and then agree on: a description of the kind of person/voice that you hear (eg style).

  d How is the readership positioned by the articles? (For example, as listener, learner, friend, conspirator etc.?)

  e What is the magazine really about? Summarise the main topics from articles and ads. Do they add up to ideas such as 'buy clothes', 'have a good time', 'wear make-up', 'you've got to be fancied', 'music is what life is about'? Look at your list of ideas and work out who would be interested in addressing you in this way.

2 Conduct an audience profile survey for one example of a quiz show. Use a variety of sources such as industry research, random interviews, questionnaires.

  The profile approaches and results could be framed in terms of examples such as socio-economic groups, lifestyle groups, gender/age/occupation, and so on.

1 What are the arguments and the evidence for the media functioning as an agency for creating passivity among social groups, or in society as a whole?
2 How far does the uses-and-gratifications theory relate to views of media influence which include ideology?
3 Evaluate one research approach which has concluded that television affects violent behaviour and attitudes in society.

1 Use ethnographic research methods to evaluate social situations and viewing behaviours as factors in young children's attitudes towards some specific programme(s) for their age group.
2 Use contrasting methods to evaluate the depiction and understanding of power in examples of comics for young people. For example, make your own content analysis of the kinds of authority figure and the kinds of power wielded in the stories. Contrast this with responses from a structured discussion with individuals and/or focus groups of young people who have read the comics.

FURTHER READING

Those books marked * are particularly accessible to students as introductions to a range of topics, but will not necessarily provide all the depth needed for properly researched essays and coursework.

O'Sullivan, T, Hartley, J, Saunders, D, Montgomery, M, & Fiske, J (1994) *Key Concepts in Communication & Cultural Studies* (3rd ed), Routledge, London.
A fairly definitive dictionary of terms, meanings and cross references.

*Burton, G (1997) *More Than Meets the Eye: an introduction to Media Studies* (2nd ed), Arnold
Structured around a process approach using key concepts, with chapter summaries, activities and useful supporting information.

*O'Sullivan, T, Dutton, B, & Rayner, P (1994) *Studying the Media*, Arnold
Structured around key concepts in media and includes case studies and activities.

ed. Briggs, A, & Cobley, P (1998) *The Media: an introduction*, Longman
A look at the state of a good range of media industries, as well as critical views of the media covering areas such as representation.

*Barrat, D (1986) *Media Sociology*, Routledge
In spite of its age, this remains a useful compact student-friendly text, leading into issues and debates.

ed. Curran, J, & Gurevitch, M (1996) *Mass media & Society*, Arnold
A useful collection of essays about the media, which may be used selectively.

Thwaites, T, Davis, L, & Mules, W (1994) *Tools for Cultural Studies*, Macmillan Australia
A well structured text for students which explains areas such as semiotics with helpful examples.

Storey, J (1997) *Cultural Theory & Popular Culture*, Prentice Hall
Quite dense, but covers a lot of historical and critical ground in the field.

*Trowler, P (1991) *Investigating the Media*, Collins
Useful coverage of key topics, but especially useful for going into methodologies of research.

Curran, J, & Seaton, J (1997) *Power without Responsibility*, Routledge
Effectively covers the development of the Press and of Broadcasting, and the state of their institutions, as well as debates about these media.

Hartley, J (1989) *Understanding News*, Routledge
A comprehensive critique of news production and news output.

McNair, B (1994) *News and Journalism in the UK*, Routledge

ed. Hall, S (1997) *Representation*, Open University/Sage
Sophisticated and definitive, this text is best used selectively.

Osgerby, B (1998) *Youth in Britain since 1945*, Blackwell
An invaluable survey of youth cultures and critical thinking about these cultures.

Morley, D (1992) *Television Audiences & Cultural Studies*, Routledge
Looks at ways of making sense of audiences, including through gender, ideology and methodologies.

Philo, G (1990) *Seeing & Believing*, Routledge
A look at media effects and issues of bias [mainly TV] by a member of the Glasgow University Media Group.

BIBLIOGRAPHY

Adorno, T (1991) *The Culture Industry*, Routledge

Althusser, L (1969) *For Marx*, Blackwell Verso

Barker, M and Petley, J (1997) *Ill Effects*, Routledge

Barthes, R (1957) *Mythologies*, Vintage

Benjamin, W (1973) *Illuminations*, Fontana

Blain, N and Boyle, R (1998) *The Media* (ed. Briggs, A. and Cobley, P), Longman

Blumler, J and Katz, E (1974) *The Uses of Mass Communication*, Sage, Beverly Hills

Boyd-Barrett, O (1995) *Approaches to Media*, Arnold

Brake, M (1985) *Comparative Youth Culture*, Routledge

Briggs, A and Cobley, P (1998) *The Media: An Introduction*, Longman

Chibnall, S (1977) *Law and Order News*, Tavistock

Cohen, S (1997) *Rethinking the Youth Question*, Macmillan

Curran, J (1996) *Cultural Studies and Communications*, Arnold

Du Gay, P et al (1997) *Doing Cultural Studies*, Sage Publications Ltd

Fiske, J (1982) *Key Concepts in Communication*, Routledge

Fiske, J (1987) *Television Culture*, Routledge

Fiske, J (1989) *Understanding Popular Culture*, Routledge

Fornas, J (1995) *Youth Culture in Late Modernity*, Sage Publications Ltd

Galtung, J and Ruge, M (1970) *Media Sociology* (ed. Tunstall, J), Constable

Ganetz, H (1995) *Youth Culture in Late Modernity*, Sage Publications Ltd

Garratt, D (1997) *Youth in Society*, Sage Publications Ltd/Open University

Gauntlett, D (1998) *Approaches to Audiences*, Arnold

Gerbner, G (1969) 'Towards Cultural Indicators', *Audio Visual Communication Review*, 17

Giddens, A (1994) *Beyond Left and Right: The future of radical politics*, Polity Press

Glasgow University Media Groups (1982) *Bad News*

Graddol, D and Boyd-Barratt, O (1994) *Media Texts, Authors and Readers*, Multilingual Matters

Gramsci, A (1971) *Selections from the Prison Notebooks*, Lawrench and Wishart

Hall, S (1981) *Culture, Media, Language*, Routledge

Hall, S (1997) *Representation: Cultural Representations and Practices*, Sage Publications Ltd

Hall, S et al (1978) *Policing the Crisis*, Macmillan Press

Hartley, J (1982) *Understanding News*, Routledge

Hebdige, D (1979) *Subculture: the Meaning of Style*, Routledge

Hodge, B and Tripp, D (1986) *Children and Television*, Stanford University Press

Hoggart, R (1958) *The Uses of Literacy*, Penguin Books

Horkheimer, M and Adorno, T (1972) *Dialectic of Enlightenment*, Blackwell Verso

Katz, E and Lazarfeld, P (1995) *Approaches to Media* (ed. Boyd-Barrett, O and Newbold, C), Arnold

Kellner, D (1991) *The Persian Gulf TV War*, Westview Press

Levi-Strauss, C (1963) *Structural Anthropology*, Basic Books

Lorimer, R (1994) *Mass Communications*, Manchester University Press

McQuail, D (1983), *Mass Communication Theory*, Sage Publications Ltd

McQuail, D (1996) *Mass Communication and Society*, Sage Publications Ltd

McRobbie, A (1994) *Postmodernism and Popular Culture*, Routledge

Milliband, R (1973) *The State in Capitalist Society*, Quartet Books

Morley, D (1980) *The Nationwide Audience*, Routledge

Morley, D (1992) *Television, Audiences and Cultural Studies*, Routledge

Morley, D (1996) *Cultural Studies and Communication*, Routledge

Mulvey, L (1975) *Visual Pleasure and Narrative Cinema*, Screen

Murdock, G and Golding, P (1997) *The Political Economy of the Media*, Edward Elgar

Negrine, R (1994) *Politics and the Mass Media in Britain*, Routledge

Negrine, R (1996) *The Communication of Politics*, Sage Publications Ltd

Nightingale, V (1996) *Studying the Television Audience*, Routledge

O'Halloran, J et al (1970) *Demonstrations and Communication*, Penguin

Osgerby, B (1997) *Youth in Britain since 1945*, Blackwell

Bourdieu, P (1984) *Distinction*, Harvard University Press

Radway, J (1984) *Reading the Romance*, Blackwell Verso

Said, E (1995) *Orientalism*, Penguin Books

Schlesinger, P (1978) *Putting Reality Together*, Constable

Schudson, M (1996) *Mass Media and Society* (ed. Curran, J and Gurevitch, M), Arnold

Seiter et al (1991) *Remote Control*, Routledge

Selby, K and Cowdery, R (1995) *How to Study Television*, Macmillan Press Ltd

Silverstone, R (1994) *Television and Everyday Life*, Routledge

Sreberny-Mohammadi, A (1996) *Mass Media and Society* (ibid.), Arnold

Strinati, D (1995) *Introduction to Theories of Popular Culture*, Routledge

Strinati, D and Wagg, S (1992) *Come on Down*, Routledge

ed. Thomson, K (1997), *Media and Cultural Regulation*, Sage Publications Ltd

Tuchman, G (1978) *Making News*, Macmillan USA

Turner, G (1990) *British Cultural Studies*, Routledge

Van Zoonen, L (1994) *Feminist Media Studies*, Sage Publications Ltd

Von Feilitzen, C (1998) *Approaches to Audience* (ed. Gauntlett, D), Arnold

Williams, G (1996) *Britain's Media*, Campaign for Press and Broadcasting Freedom

Williams, R (1961) *The Long Revolution*, Hogarth Press

Williams, R (1974) *Television, Technology and Cultural Form*, Wesleyan University Press

Wright, C (1960) 'Functional Inventory', *Analysis of Mass Communication*, Public Opinion Quarterly, vol 24

INDEX

ACCESS TO POLITICS

Access to Politics is a series of concise and readable topic books for politics students. Each book provides advice on note-taking, tackling exam questions, developing skills of analysis, evaluation and presentation, and reading around the subject.

TITLES PUBLISHED IN 1998:

UK Government and Politics in Context	0340 71134 5
Protecting Rights in Britain	0340 71136 1
Local and Regional Government in Britain	0340 71184 1
Voting Behaviour and Electoral Systems	0340 71135 3
British Politics and Europe	0340 72079 4

TITLES PUBLISHING IN 1999:

The Prime Minister and Cabinet Government	0340 74759 5
Pressure Groups	0340 74758 7
The Environment and British Politics	0340 74791 9
The Government and the Economy	0340 74278 X
Law, Order and the Judiciary	0340 75772 8

See page iv for information on how to order copies.